# EARLY
# CANADIAN
# GLASS

## Gerald Stevens

Gerald Stevens is the author of *The Canadian Collector* and *Canadian Glass*
*c.1825-1925*, both published by Coles Publishing Company.

Cover glassware courtesy of Whimsy Antiques, Toronto, Ontario.

## TO EDITH,

without whose help and encouragement excavation in earth and archives would have been impossible.

# FOREWORD

Gerald Stevens has become one of the leading experts and collectors in the field of Canadiana. His interests and intimate knowledge cover a wide range, from painting and pewter, furniture and firearms, to old silver and early Canadian glass. In the highly specialized field of early Canadian glass he has become pre-eminent, and is regarded in Canada and abroad as our outstanding authority.

*Early Canadian Glass* takes its place as a landmark book. It is the logical culmination of a lifetime of connoisseurship that began as a young man in the Stevens Art Gallery, Montreal, founded by his father, and in which he became partner and later owner. His recent book, *Frederick Simpson Coburn, R.C.A.* (1958), was a memorial to one of his oldest clients and friends. Upon retiring from the Stevens Art Gallery he and his wife purchased a farm with a lovely old stone house near Mallorytown, Ontario, and this has since become a private museum, and a mecca for the serious amateur collector as well as the professional.

Gerald Stevens put down his first thoughts on Canadiana—the collecting of beautiful farmsteads—in his first book, *The Old Stone House* (1954), and its logical successor, *In a Canadian Attic*, appeared the following year. In 1957 he published *The Canadian Collector*, devoted to glass, pottery, furniture and firearms, with an Introduction by Mr. F. St. George Spendlove, Curator of the Canadiana Collections, Royal Ontario Museum. This established Gerald Stevens as the principal authority on early Canadian glass. The present volume grows out of all that went before, out of years of research and authenticating, on-the-spot digging, and collecting. In all this his wife was an enthusiastic and perceptive colleague.

*Early Canadian Glass* reviews briefly the art and craft of glass-making from earliest times, and quickly comes to the author's main theme, glass-making in early Nineteenth Century Canada. All the known glass houses of Canada are considered, by regions and in detail, the products in which they specialized, the sources of their raw materials, with comment on design, social and industrial needs, and on leading executives and craftsmen.

*Early Canadian Glass* is the first general summary of whatever is known, and can reasonably be authenticated, about early Canadian glass. Nothing is withheld from the connoisseur or student that has any relevance. If little or nothing can be said, as in the case with the almost mythical glass works at Cayuga, Ontario, then little or nothing will be said. Certainly there are no guesses, inspired or otherwise. For the rest Gerald Stevens gives the actual site of the glass works, its period of active operation, and the names of the management, the foremen, blowers, finishers, porters, packers and general workmen when known. He also lists the known products of the glass works, the quality and colour of the glass made, and he is specific about decoration, and design, as well as about cutting, engraving, gilding and sand blasting—everything, in fact, that would assist the collector to place and authenticate a find.

There are many human interest touches in this historical handbook, from the fabulous Mr. Smith and his fancy glass curiosities (1840), and the amazing John Herring of Napanee (1881-1883), to William Godkin Beach, who bridged top management in both Hamilton, Ontario, and Trenton, Nova Scotia. Then there are the unique blowers of paperweights—William McGinnis, George Mullin, Patrick Wickham, George Gardiner and others.

Since the publication of his historical and descriptive *Catalogue*, of The Edith Chown Pierce and Gerald Stevens Collection of Early Canadian Glass, Royal Ontario Museum, (1957) he has increased his detailed study of Canadian glass works from five to seventeen, and has untangled the complicated histories of several, including Ottawa Glass Works, Canada Glass Works, Hudson, Quebec, The Foster Brothers, St. Johns, Quebec, and others. He has also indicated where the intensive quest will be made by the collector of the future—the special creations of the leading glass blowers, drapes, witch balls and canes and other novelties, and such whimsies as hats, hatchets, swords, hammers and paperweights.

No longer will the glass works at Mallorytown be referred to as a bit of possible folklore, or the pioneer glass houses of Burlington, the Seigniory of Vaudreuil, or Trenton, Nova Scotia, lack a local habitation, and a proud name in history.    No longer will the Canadian collector and connoisseur look for a George McKearin to put the known data in order, and provide clues for the ready identification and authentication of the products of our glass works that have been making history for 135 years.

*Early Canadian Glass* has been solidly based upon all known sources of published and archival data, and on personal correspondence with families of early management and pioneer glass workers.    The author and his wife have explored the sites of early glass works, working patiently over slag heaps and deposits of waste.    Every available specimen of early Canadian glass in public or private collections has been examined.    The author and his wife will continue to explore glass works sites and our archives, and they will continue to collect representative specimens of early Canadian glass, chiefly 1825-1890.    This book is the first complete summing up of all known and authenticated data, and no doubt it will be revised as time goes on.    More glass works may be discovered, and more may be learned about glass works already well known, their products and their chief artisans.    This book will remain as the standard authority for museums and collectors, antique dealers and historians.    As time goes on Gerald Stevens and his wife will be adding important specimens to the Collection in the Royal Ontario Museum, maintaining it as the principal one of its kind in the world.    His name will be permanently identified in all works of reference as the principal historian and collector in this rare, highly specialized and altogether fascinating division of Canadiana—early Canadian glass.

LORNE PIERCE

# The Evolution of Sheet Glass Making

## CROWN GLASS

This was the first method of manufacturing sheets of glass through which clear vision could be obtained. The glass was gathered at the end of a blowpipe and blown into a pear-shaped form. An iron rod, on the end of which was a blob of hot glass, was then pressed against the thick end of the pear to which it stuck, and the neck of the pear holding the pipe broken off. The remaining portion was re-heated and by spinning it was opened out into the form of a disc about four feet in diameter, which was cut into small panes.

## SHEET GLASS—CYLINDER BLOWN

Another early process was Cylinder Blown in which a long glass bubble was blown and shaped into cylindrical form. The ends were opened and cut off, and the resulting cylinder split length ways. Placed in a heated chamber, it softened again and was flattened into a sheet with the aid of a wooden tool held on an iron rod. Ripples in the glass were straight and not circular as in the Crown process.

## PLATE GLASS—TABLE CAST

The fact that distortion in the glass produced by these early methods made it unsuitable for mirrors led to the first manufacture of plate glass by the French towards the end of the 17th century. Molten glass was poured from the melting pot on to an iron table to form a thin slab. Because of the contact with the metal it lost its fire-finished surfaces. So the slab had to be ground and polished with abrasives to get true, parallel surfaces.

## PLATE GLASS—TWIN GRINDER

The most recent glass-making development before the Float process was the Twin Grinder invented by Pilkington Brothers in 1937 for the manufacture of plate glass. A continuous ribbon of glass 100 inches wide travels at 200 inches a minute between grinding heads above and below, for more than 1,000 feet. To-day, this is the standard plate glass machine in every major glass making country except Russia and Japan.

*The four illustrations, with the accompanying text, are used with the permission of Pilkington Brothers.

No. 2.

# INTRODUCTION

## GLASS-MAKING AND GLASS-MAKERS

A technically accurate and completely documented history of glass-making in Canada has yet to be written. The author hopes that the present work will inspire further efforts in this field of Canadiana.

It is difficult to picture a twentieth century without glass in its many forms: no electric light as we know it today, no bottles, drinking glasses, pyrex accessories for the kitchen, preserving jars, test tubes, retorts, and other laboratory apparatus, and no glass windows.

Authoritative writers on glass have obtained their data from personal research, ancient chronicles and commentaries and modern archaeological discoveries. By these means they have established a surprisingly accurate history of the evolution of the designs and techniques used by artisans to manufacture glass, from about 2000 B.C. down to the time of mechanization in 1915.

Pliny the Younger (c.61-c.113) records the tradition that glass was discovered accidentally by sailors driven upon the coast of Phoenicia. While they were cooking their meal, the story goes, alkali fused with sand and so made a glaze. Although modern authorities question this tradition, it is possible that glass-making was known in Egypt before 1800 B.C. The Egyptians were not only acquainted with glass, but knew how to stain it with various colours, and produce articles with extraordinary skill. The art of producing transparent glass was a later development, and very high values were placed upon vessels of clear glass. Drinking vessels, flagons and window glasses were ultimately produced in Italy, Spain and elsewhere, but were invariably the property of the well-to-do. India and China likewise have histories of interest to the connoisseur of old glass. Venetians were the first Europeans to achieve distinction in glass-making, and shipped window glass to Britain in the fourteenth and fifteenth centuries for use in churches. It was so excessively rare and costly that, as late as 1567, the window glass of Alnwick Castle was placed in the casements when the lord of the manor arrived, and removed for safekeeping when he left.    Glass slowly took the place of wicker-work and lattice made of oak laths, and was in general use not earlier than 1700 in Great Britain.

The technique of blowing and shaping glass by skilled glass blowers is treated at length in many available books, and in articles in standard reference works.   The techniques employed and the skills required in the leading glass houses abroad were those used in the glass houses of Canada. Casual reference will be made to these techniques and skills in the present work in so far as they affect the description or authentication of examples of early Canadian glass.   For the rest the reader is referred to specialized texts indicated in the bibliography at the end of this book.

As time has gone on, the needs of mass production prevail.   The skilled individual in Canada, the artist with the blowpipe and the pontil rod or "ponty," has all but disappeared.   Mr. E. G. Davies, manager of the Dominion Glass Company, Limited at Wallaceburg, Ontario, states in a letter to the author dated January 14, 1959: "There are no (glass) blowers being employed in Canada at the present time.   Our last hand-blowing operation at this plant was about 1942."

It is unwise to date glass by technique alone.   There is a good deal of confusion about the introduction of methods of various kinds in glass works in North America.   A point of interest, especially for the amateur collector, is that the later types of moulded (pressed) glass bearing names and dates are not necessarily of an age indicated by the date.   Classic examples of this dating may be seen on Plate No. 38, and Plate No. 3.   The first of these, the *Queen Victoria, 1837, clear glass cake or bread plate* was manufactured in several Canadian glass houses *circa* 1890-1910.   It is quite possible that the original design for the mould predates the twentieth century by many years, but the date of 1837 moulded in the glass is merely copied from the inscription of the portrait used as a decoration. The second of the pieces, the *Marquis and Marchioness of Lorne pitcher*, is also a product of Canadian glass houses.   Although this is said to have been made in England it was produced in Canada in the 1890's.   The specimen shown here is made from marble glass or, as it is known in the antique trade, purple slag.   Such pieces may be found in both clear and

No. 3.  Pitcher pressed in a three-section mould in glass of the type
known as blue (purple) slag.  Earlier version—blue—white opal glass.
This is the well-known Marquis of Lorne design, often attributed to
English glass houses but now known to have been produced in several
Canadian houses—particularly those in Nova Scotia and Ontario.

coloured glass, and were made to commemorate the arrival of the Governor General and his lady in Nova Scotia in 1878. Again, this mould may have been first used in 1878, but it was certainly used in the last decade of the nineteenth century. The term marble glass is correct, as this was the type of glass used for the glass marbles or alleys so popular with children. Indeed, several of these playthings and chunks of glass from which they were made have been excavated on the site of The Burlington Glass Works in Hamilton, Ontario.

As the majority of glass objects presently available to collectors of Canadiana were manufactured by moulding or pressing, it interested this writer to learn that the art of moulding glass was understood in Egypt.

The early histories of glass-making stress the importance of two types of glass; window glass, both functional and ornamental, and glass vessels used as containers.

Both glass-making and glass-moulding were first discovered by Egyptians who moulded small, brilliantly coloured glass jars and bottles, and presented them to dark-eyed charmers who used these novelties as containers for perfume, ungents and cosmetics. Egyptian ladies of the period understood the allure of eyelids darkened and emphasized by the use of kohl, and glass vessels complete with spatulas thought to have been containers for this and similar beauty aids have been excavated in modern times. All of these containers are opaque. Many of the designs would be considered today as ultra-modern.

These phials, jugs and ewers are today listed as alabastra, amphoroe and œnochoe. Canadians are fortunate indeed that collections of this early glass may be studied at the Royal Ontario Museum, Toronto, and at The Montreal Museum of Fine Arts. The Toronto collection was donated by Miss Helen Norton, and that in Montreal, which is the finest in Canada, by Mr. Harry A. Norton.

Miss Ruth Jackson, custodian of records at The Montreal Museum of Fine Arts, has supplied the following information relative to the latter collection.

The Norton Collection of Ancient Glass consists of 163 pieces. The earliest examples date *circa* 1500 B.C., and were manufactured by the method known as core wound. Of a later period, Roman, are specimens of the extremely beautiful mosaic and millefiori types. Of a still later time are jars dating from the fourth century after Christ. About these last specimens Miss Jackson has this to say:

These are all very similar, and were originally thought to have been made in the Seine-Rhine area. Later investigation has shown numbers from Palestinian excavations, and if they were made in the area they were almost certainly produced by Syrian glass workers who had emigrated there.

A condensed listing of some of the rarer items in the Norton Collection would include:

A *cinerary urn* with cover, Roman, late first or second century after Christ; a *flask* having a base of twin cherub heads, Roman, *circa* A.D. 150; a Constantinean period *flask* with a Christian symbol apparently meant to represent a full-length figure of Christ; a *drinking horn*, undecorated, northwestern Europe, dating A.D. 400-600. There are also *flasks* of Roman marbled ware, *mould-blown flasks* from Sidonia and Syria dating 100 B.C.-A.D. 100, and in particular a *blue mosque lamp* of the fourteenth century. This special item bears the inscription "Made by the Order of His Excellency Tu Su, the Bey of Sham, in the time of the Exalted, The Lord, The King, The Master Saif Addin an Nasir." (A Mamaluk Sultan of Egypt and Syria of the Bahri Dynasty, 1345-1346.)

The technique used to produce these early containers was a type of moulding, and unlike the later methods this was the work of several hours. Taking a metal rod (the progenitor of the pontil rod), the workman gathered fine strands from a melting pot and wound these strands one by one around a core or mould of sand. When the glass had cooled —was it annealed?—the sand was washed and scraped away, and the completed piece was made available to the wealthy. The ancient glassmakers used a second technique, similar in result. By this method the sand core was dipped again and again into the molten batch of metal. Thus layer after layer of glass was added, each layer of glass being shaped and worked by a wooden paddle in a manner quite similar to that used by nineteenth century glass-workers creating a paperweight.

Strange as it may seem, the invention of the blowpipe came after the discovery of moulding. It was not until the third century B.C. that the blowpipe came into general use. With the advent of the blowpipe the technique known as blown-moulded (called mould-blown in England) was introduced. This allowed an almost unlimited number of forms to be adapted to glass manufacture, and the Romans perfected and used many new types and utensils made of glass.

During this period, covering almost a thousand years, all glass was coloured, not by intent but by necessity. The earliest glass had been discovered in white, purple, brown, blue, and yellow. The Romans added such colours as green and amber.

By the tenth century the cutting wheel was in use, and mould-blown containers decorated with wheel-cutting have been discovered. This glass is credited to Islam, and Islamic glass dominates the field of glass-making up to the thirteenth century after Christ. The sixteenth century found the glass blowers of Venice supreme in technique and decoration. Moulds of more than one piece were introduced, and such complicated techniques as *latticinio* glass were being used.

The Renaissance, that revival of arts and letters in the fifteenth century, had introduced the art of glass-making throughout Europe. Within a short period the Rhineland and Antwerp were competing with Venice, and by the latter half of the sixteenth century these centres, along with the Low Countries and Spain, were manufacturing glass for the commoner as well as for the nobility.

The seventeenth century was, from the viewpoint of the collector of North American glass, the most important era in the history of glass-making; the first glass house in the New World had produced glass.

There is a strange similarity between the history of the first glass house in North America and that of the first glass house in Canada. Both locations were unmarked, and the plough and grazing cattle obliterated all traces. The Jamestown glass works were founded in a newly won part of the British Empire, and the Mallorytown house was established by United Empire Loyalists and their descendants.

The story of the Jamestown venture is preserved in the writings of its leader, Captain John Smith who, financed by the London Company, landed at Jamestown, Virginia, in 1607. This first group of pioneers was followed by a second which included eight glass-makers. These "Dutch and Poles" erected a small glass house, and within a short period "glasse" was being shipped to England.

Discoveries on the site of the Jamestown glass works show that this had been a serious attempt at glass manufacture. Excavation has unearthed many glass fragments, melting pots, a cullet pile, several types of furnaces, and part of a working hole. The written records suggest that glass was made from 1608 to 1609, but that manufacture was then discontinued. In 1621-1622, a Captain William Norton arrived with six glass blowers from Italy, and glass-making was again attempted. This was a success, and fires remained burning until 1624. In that year this first and very gallant attempt to introduce an ancient art to North America came to an end.

Canada is increasing in stature, and in the future, as in the past, our maturity will be attested by the work of our artists and artisans. Less than three decades ago Canadian art was considered unimportant, and early Canadian glass was thought to be mythical. Today a Canadian painting will fetch $20,000 or more, while Canadian glass is recognized in Canada, England and the United States as worthy of the attention of the collector and the connoisseur. The future holds much promise for the study of Canadiana, but only if Canadians themselves show an interest in the early arts and crafts of their own country. Can we not follow the lead of Henry Ford who purchased the Farrar pottery of St. Johns, Quebec, and moved it to the United States as an "Early American" pottery, or of George McKearin who purchased the first piece of Canadian glass and listed it as such in his *American Glass?* Must we always depend on researchers from other countries? The present work shows that Canadian glass houses produced vast quantities of almost every type of glass manufactured during the nineteenth century, and that individual glass blowers made whimseys and special pieces equal in merit to those produced by the general run of glass workers in other countries.

Interest in Canadiana in general and Canadian glass in particular is growing. A pooling of such data on early Canadian glass as can be authenticated in some manner could be effected by sending them to any of the following: the author, Mallorytown, Ontario; the Royal Ontario Museum, Toronto, Ontario; the Montreal Museum of Fine Arts, Montreal, Quebec. The data thus received could be cross-checked and, if correct, incorporated into the record of which this present work is only the beginning.

# CONTENTS

*Contents*

# LIST OF ILLUSTRATIONS

# 1 *The Glass Houses of Ontario*

# 1 *The Glass Houses of Ontario*

## 1. THE MALLORY GLASS WORKS, MALLORYTOWN (*circa* 1825, 1839-1840)

IT WAS NOT until August 22, 1953, that the Canadian public learned that glass had been manufactured in Canada prior to the twentieth century.

This important disclosure was delayed because of certain historical conditions. During the nineteenth century, Canada had remained colonial in outlook, and had turned to the Mother Country, England, for inspiration in the arts and crafts. Wealthy people of Canada sought only those *objects d'art* guaranteed to be imported; their paintings, china, glass, furniture, textiles, and so on, all came from abroad. Furthermore Canada was adjacent to a highly developed nation whose critics and historians paid scant attention to the accomplishments of their sparsely populated neighbour to the north. Most Canadians remained convinced that their own accomplishments were negligible. It was only the rare individual who insisted that Canada had contributed something to the world's culture.

With the advent of the twentieth century this conviction of inferiority began to be questioned. Canadian painters, writers, poets and artisans began to gain recognition. People began to ask questions. Why had so many branches of Canadian crafts, such as glass-making, been ignored? Could a company of the importance of Dominion Glass have sprung full fledged from nothing? Had *any* glass been manufactured in Canada in the nineteenth century?

No. 4.  Sugar Bowl and Cover: Deep aquamarine.  Made at
Mallorytown Glass House (*Circa* 1825).

Here and there about the country there were people who had the answers; but they either were uninterested or had expressed themselves only in casual papers or in articles in publications having a very limited circulation. In the United States such authorities as George and Helen McKearin and Ruth Webb Lee had written on American glass without making any distinction between Canada and the United States. All of these experts had mentioned a glass house at Mallorytown, but had treated this attempt to manufacture glass in Canada more or less as folk-lore. The McKearins illustrated a pitcher and gave its source as Mallorytown, but their text identifies Mallorytown as "a hamlet in the Province of Quebec." Ruth Webb Lee suggested that the pattern of pressed glass listed as Canadian was possibly a product of this Canadian glass house, but left the reader wondering. The truth is, all authorities were affected by the apathetic approach of Canadians themselves to their own attainments in the arts and crafts.

Through such hints, at any rate, it became known that glass was made at Mallorytown, Ontario, at what may be considered an early date in the British regime in Canada. It is even possible that glass was produced in Canada during the French regime but there is no proven record of this. If such is found to be true, it will be a most important discovery.

It was the discovery of the site of the Mallorytown glass works that inaugurated an investigation into glass-making in Canada, and led ultimately to the writing of this book. The author had retired to a farm-house situated in the environs of the village of Mallorytown, and being interested in Americana and Canadiana of every type, including glass (the latter interest having been inspired by the late Mr. Harry A. Norton, the dean of Canadian glass collectors), acquired the previously mentioned works on American glass. These aroused in him a determination to prove or disprove the existence of the legendary glass house at Mallorytown. Preliminary investigations were made, and it was discovered that several pieces of glass owned by local residents were claimed to have been made at Mallorytown. Further inquiries revealed that several digging expeditions had taken place, financed from American and Canadian sources. The names of the diggers and their backers could not be dis-covered, but the results were known to be negative. The consensus was that the Mallorytown glass house was merely a figment of the imagination, and that the glass found in the Mallorytown area had been made in either the Redwood or Redford glass houses in northern New York State.

Investigations covering several years and seven different sites finally led to an interview with Mr. Fred Guild and his brother Lawrence in which they indicated the correct location. With this vital information, we prepared to dig.

On August 18, 1953, Mr. Fred Guild and his brother Lawrence with tractor and two-furrow plough, and Mrs. Stevens and I with our shovel and rake, went to work. The information supplied to Mr. Guild by his grandfather was authenticated when, within six inches, the plough exposed several small pieces of aquamarine-coloured glass. Further ploughing, digging and brushing revealed many pieces of glass, glass gall, threads, portions of melting pots, hand-wrought nails, a coin dated 1816, and shards of worked glass.

The discovery aroused some interest locally, and the next day we were requested to re-enact our operations for the local press. The following day *The Recorder and Times* of Brockville, Ontario, published an illustrated article on the find. This publicity attracted the attention of authorities and collectors. Dr. G. F. G. Stanley of the Royal Military College, Kingston, representing the Historic and Archaeological Sites Board of Ontario, visited the site. Mr. F. St. George Spendlove, curator of the Canadiana Collections at the Royal Ontario Museum, interviewed the writer and made a written report to the Sites Board.

Dr. Lorne Pierce and his wife, the late Edith Chown Pierce, also visited the diggings. Both Dr. Pierce and Mrs. Pierce were noted collectors of Canadiana, and Mrs. Pierce was keenly interested in Canadian glass. This visit was the occasion of a meeting which resulted in the forming of the most important Collection of Early Canadian Glass, the Edith Chown Pierce and Gerald Stevens Collection in the Royal Ontario Museum, Toronto.

The discovery inspired both official notice and editorial comment in the press, and resulted in several articles by the present writer, including one entitled "Early Canadian Glass" in *Historic Kingston*, *No. 3*, (the

No. 5.  Discovery of a section of melting pot; site of the Mallorytown Glass Works.  *Left to right:* The author, Mr. Fred Guild (with shard), Mrs. Stevens, Mr. Lawrence Guild.

yearly publication of the Kingston Historical Society, Kingston, Ontario), and a privately printed brochure, *Canadian Glass: A Footnote to History* by Edith Chown Pierce.

Although the existence of the Mallorytown glass house had now become a proven fact, it remained undocumented for several years. Every effort was made to discover some mention of this establishment. Property deeds were searched, early records of the district were sought out, university libraries were contacted, without any written or printed record being unearthed.

Elderly persons or those interested in local history were interviewed, and were asked to commit themselves either orally or in writing to estimates of the dates of this glass house.

The oldest person to be interviewed was the late Mr. John Dixie, then in his 103rd year. I asked Mr. Dixie if he had been a lifelong resident of the area. He replied that he had been born in Ballycanoe in 1850. (Ballycanoe is a parish approximately six miles north of the village of Mallorytown). We next questioned him as to whether or not a glass house had been operative during his lifetime. His answer was, "Not during my time, but I heard my father speak of it." This established the fact that the glass works had ceased to operate before 1850.

We then visited Mrs. Rosanna Purvis, aged 86. According to her the site of the glass works was just a pasture during her lifetime. Mrs. Purvis stated that her family had owned a bottle (broken in 1931) said by her husband's grandfather (1799-1890) to have been made at Mallory-town. Mrs. Purvis's estimate of the date of the factory was 1820. These notes were written down, signed by Mrs. Rosanna Purvis and witnessed by Mrs. Kathleen Purvis.

Additional signed and witnessed statements were obtained from Mrs. Henrietta Lilly Guild, Mr. Fred Guild and Mr. Lawrence Guild.

Mrs. Guild (aged 86 in 1953) stated that the field was just a field in her lifetime, and that there were no evidences of buildings whatsoever, but that her husband's father had spoken of the factory.

Mr. Fred Guild (the one person knowing the correct location) stated that he had been shown the location by his grandfather (Elbin Guild), who took him to the site and, after pointing it out, told him that the field had held only signs of a foundation and a well when he was a young boy. The grandfather had estimated the date of the glass works as 1825. This statement was signed by Messrs. Fred and Lawrence Guild, co-workers on the excavations.

In quest of further information, documented if possible, and of un-broken worked specimens of glass manufactured at Mallorytown, we asked the local newspapers to insert advertisements. Many answers

*Courtesy The Recorder Printing Co. Ltd., Brockville, Ont.*

No. 6.   A bird's-eye view of the site of the Mallorytown Glass Works.
*Left to right:* Mr. Fred Guild, Miss Betty McDowell (feature writer for
*The Recorder* and *Times*), the author, Mrs. Edith
Stevens, and Mr. Lawrence Guild.

were received.  Some were relevant, and the writers were interviewed.
In this way we discovered several specimens and, after thorough investigation of both sources and pieces, added them to a growing collection.  Few
though these pieces were, they were of prime importance.  The district
had been combed for many years by antique dealers who, if they did
obtain authentic examples, credited the greater part to American glass
houses, the best known exception being the lily-pad pitcher in the
collection of Mr. George McKearin.

In addition to acquiring specimens of glass, we obtained some
descriptions of pieces that "had been in the family but had been lost or
discarded" that were repeated so often that particulars were noted for
future reference on the chance that examples described would be encountered.  This circumstance was indeed fortunate, for at a much later
date (1957) it brought about the authentication and acquisition of the
so-far unique doorstop-paperweight.  Authentication of early glass is
most difficult and requires great care.  We therefore requested one of the
people who had several years before described such doorstops to supple-
ment oral information in writing.  We are indebted to Mrs. B. Ford
(Kathleen) Purvis for the following letter:

> The green glass doorstop with bits of white, blue and red glass inside,
> is the same as several used in old houses around Mallorytown, and the
> colour is exactly similar to that of a bottle obtained from the old glass
> works by Great-Grandfather George Purvis.

The years intervening between the first serious attempt at research
on Canadian glass and the present time (1960) have not been completely
wasted.  Assisted at first by (Mrs.) Edith Chown Pierce and later by
Dr. Lorne Pierce, we continued to gather data.  Many Canadian glass
houses were documented with the aid of nineteenth century directories,
reports and newspapers, but no mention of the Mallorytown works was
encountered.  The reference librarians of such libraries as those of Queen's
University, McGill University, the National Archives, the Hamilton
Public Library and the University of Toronto assisted in the search; but
the stacks revealed nothing concerning the first Canadian glass house.
Existence of the glass works at Mallorytown had been proven by excava-

*Courtesy The Recorder Printing Co. Ltd., Brockville, Ont.*

No. 7.　Burnham Bowl and Cover, Shards, Chunks of Glass, Sections of Melting Pots, etc. photographed the day following the proving of the Mallorytown Glass works.

tion, but the name of the owner and the date when it ceased operation remained a mystery.

It was not until the autumn of 1958 that the answers to these questions were received.

Mr. Ernest I. Miller of Mallorytown is interested in local history. This is only natural, as his great-grandfather, William Miller, was one of the early members of the Quebec Literary and Historical Society, and received a citation in 1834 from that honourable body. He moved to Mallorytown in 1836 and taught school there for many years. By good luck Mr. E. I. Miller chanced to read in an old newspaper dated 1878 an article mentioning the Mallorytown glass works, its last dates and its owner. Knowing my interest in this glass house, he drew my attention to the article, which contained the following excerpt:

A. W. (Andrew) Mallory Esq., is a gentleman of great enterprise, ready at all times to embark in any speculation in which his shrewd intelligence discerns a profitable investment. He is the son of the late

David Mallory and was born in 1819. . . . At that early age he assisted his father in lumbering . . . supplying the Kingston Penitentiary and dock yards and the Mail Line of Steamers with cordwood. At various times he has opened and successfully carried on a general store, a blacksmith shop with two forges for twenty years, *a glass factory during 1839 to '40 which was closed owing to the unreliableness of the foreman. . . .* He owns at present over 1000 acres of land. . . . In his public capacity he has been 21 years road master, 12 years a School Trustee, 9 years a Councillor, 3 years Reeve (1869, '70 and '71) and other positions of trust. Mr. Mallory has been married twice, his first wife dying in 1854, by whom he had six children, two only of whom are still living. He again married, in 1857, Miss Nancy Purvis, by whom he has had nine, seven of whom are living—a kind and indulgent husband and parent, he is almost worshipped in his family circle. His usefulness as a citizen is sufficiently attested, as is his popularity, by the brief record given above.

Andrew Mallory was the son of Nathaniel (Nathan?) Mallory, a United Empire Loyalist. The elder Mallory had settled at Mallorytown Landing in 1784, but shortly afterward moved to what was to become the village of Mallorytown (which was named for him). A most progressive man, Nathaniel proceeded to establish a cordwood business, a pack train for bringing supplies from Montreal and Kingston, a brick-yard, and several other ventures in manufacture and trade. There are two reasons for supposing that this first of the Mallorys originated the attempt at glass-making: first, the correctness of everything relative to the history of the glass house supplied by Elbin Guild; and second, the proven fact that Nathaniel Mallory's son Andrew carried on and/or revived many of his father's attempts to settle and improve the township of the Front of Yonge.

The above data were obtained from an article in a newspaper, *Our Cheerful Friend*, vol. VII, no. IV., April 1, 1879, published in Brockville, Ontario, by J. T. White, 76 Church St. The author does not vouch for the accuracy of this article. Even the most hawkeyed of proofreaders have been known to err, and the details about Andrew's children have been otherwise given by writers contemporary with Mr. White.

As far as can be ascertained by digging, the first proven Canadian glass house used local materials. These included Potsdam sandstone,

*Author's italics.

quartz, and wood-ash potash.    There is no resonance to the glass, and lead was not used as a flux.

Knowing that sandstone can be obtained locally in quantity, and that this sandstone had been used by one Canadian glass house (Napanee) to produce glass, a chemical analysis was then made at Queen's University, Kingston.    The following is an excerpt from an article entitled "Sandstone for Glass-making" in *Geology and Minerals in the County of Leeds, 31st Annual Report of the Ontario Dept. of Mines*, vol. XXXI, part VI, 1922, pages 18-19:

Believing that this pure white siliceous sandstone had possibilities in the glass and porcelain industries, also possibly for refractory linings for furnaces, the writer [M. B. Baker] collected some of this sandstone, and has made it the subject of a special investigation.    An advanced student of geology at Queen's University, J. W. Greig, was given the problem of making a physical and chemical investigation of this material, and the results of his work are summarized as follows:

"In order that a sandstone may be suitable as a source of silica for the manufacture of glass it must fulfil a number of conditions.    The most important of these is a required chemical composition.    No sand occurring in nature is pure silica, and each of the impurities affects the glass in a different way.    The most prevalent impurity is alumina($Al_2O_3$). This may be present in the sand in the form of feldspar, clay, or other aluminous silicate, in small pieces which have not been destroyed in the weathering down of the original rock, or as clay between the grains of quartz.    The latter is the more likely.    Alumina, although an impurity, is not detrimental, however, in the small quantities usually found in a glass sand, but it has the following effects on the glass.    (1) It appears to reduce the tendency of a glass to devitrify or crystallize.    (2) Three or four per cent. of alumina in a glass renders it less susceptible to the reducing effect of a flame.    (3) It reduces the coefficient of expansion of a glass.    (4) It increases the tenacity and the surface tension of the molten glass, and this is very beneficial in moulding.    (5) It increases the brilliancy, and decreases the solubility of a glass in water.    From the above points and others it will be seen that alumina not above three per cent is beneficial to a glass rather than injurious.

"The most detrimental impurity likely to be found in a sand is iron. It imparts a cream colour to the stone, and washing will frequently remove a great part of it.    Ferrous iron, even in small quantities, imparts a bluish to greenish colour to the glass.    So common is this impurity that almost any glass, in thick sections, will be seen to have a greenish cast.

This effect can often be overcome by what are called discolourizers, the most common of which is manganese dioxide. This material added to a glass imparts a violet shade, which neutralizes to some extent the green due to iron. But this neutralizing is accomplished chiefly by absorption of light rays, so that the transparency of the glass is impaired. Most authorities agree that iron should not exceed 0.05 per cent. in the sand, although the glass sands of Belgium, which are extensively used for sheet and plate glass, contain as much as 0.25 per cent of iron.

"Clay or alumina in glass is said to cause a cloudiness, and consequently any sand with a clay content which cannot be removed by washing should not be used in the manufacture of glass.

"Silica is the useful part of the sand, and the percentage should be as high as possible. Whether or not a sand is suitable for glass manufacture can be best seen by a chemical analysis showing the percentage of impurities. Most glass sands contain upwards of 97 per cent of silica. The sand grains composing the sandstone should be fairly uniform in size. On crushing, the material should break between, and among the grains, rather than across them. The size of the grains is of considerable importance. With large grains the length of time required to flux is longer, and therefore the output of the furnace is lessened. On the other hand, very fine-grained material is said to 'burn out' in the batch. Thorough mixing of the ingredients is also very difficult when the grains are very fine, and there is likely to be considerable loss from the finest sand going up the flue with the draught. The most suitable sizes of grain appear to be between 80 and 20 mesh. The grains may be either angular or rounded, and there does not appear to be any consensus of opinion as to which is the more suitable form."

The following chemical analysis of white Potsdam sandstone is given:

| $SiO_2$ | $Al_2O_3$ | $Fe_2O_3$ | MgO | CaO |
|---------|-----------|-----------|-----|-----|
| 99.45   | 0.11      | 0.13      | ....| 0.23 |

This report made by Mr. Greig is particularly interesting, as it explains the reason for the almost uniformly natural colourization occurring in authenticated pieces of worked glass produced at the Mallorytown glass house. Although excavation revealed great quantities of opaque gall-like chunks of glass, of a colour resembling a dirty olive green, any shards showing evidence of manipulation, and some quantities of aquamarine cullet, prove that this house limited its output to a bluish-green bottle glass. It has been suggested that this colour resulted from a deliberate attempt on the part of the Mallorytown glass-makers to reproduce the peculiar tint to be seen in the waters of the St. Lawrence River on a particularly brilliant day; but the fact is that the "St. Lawrence blue" colour of the glass manufactured at Mallorytown was the result of the iron content in the sand, and of this alone.

Several conclusions of a definitive nature may be drawn from the shards and fragments excavated on the site. These are: (i) all glass produced was made by the method known as "free-blown"—in other words, the Mallorytown glass-makers did not use moulds; (ii) any clear or flint glass said to have been made there must be attributed to some other source; (iii) it was a small, one-furnace house, and its production was limited to containers and whimseys. Of course, the term containers covers many shapes and forms; included would be bottles, flasks, bowls and pitchers. The term whimseys is unlimited in scope, and could include any novelty contemporary with the dates of the factory.

## AUTHENTICATED SPECIMENS

Up to the time of going to press seven pieces of Mallorytown glass have been authenticated. These are a sugar bowl and cover, a duplicate bowl and cover, a vase-like bottle, a lily-pad pitcher, a tumbler, a flask and a doorstop-paperweight. Although these are few, they are of great importance to the historical record of glass manufacturing in Canada. It is true that the McKearin collection includes a lily-pad pitcher which is a duplicate of that in the collection in the Royal Ontario Museum. This has been ascertained by a visit made by the writer to the McKearin collection in Hoosic Falls, New York. There is also the possibility that several pieces have been acquired by other collectors in the United States. The persons from which these pieces are said to have been obtained have been interviewed, however, and from their descriptions several can definitely be stated to be of much later origin. Whether or not there are pieces in the United States, *any* specimen of glass made at Mallorytown is almost unique, and comparable in rarity to the earliest silver from Quebec, or a painting by Krieghoff or Kane.*

From the historical standpoint, the sugar bowl and cover listed as the *Burnham bowl* may be said to be the most important Mallorytown item in The Edith Chown Pierce and Gerald Stevens Collection. This bowl is the best known and best documented product of that glass house. For many years the Burnham family had claimed that this piece "had been made at the old glass works in the village." Indeed this claim— presented in a confident manner—was the *raison d'être* for the prolonged search to establish whether this lost glass house was fact or fiction. Everyone in the Mallorytown district knew of this bowl, and several collectors had left standing offers for it with the family. It is an interesting but not unique specimen of early glass when judged on its own merits. But as an example of early Canadian glass it is outstanding. Not only is it claimed by the Burnham family to have been manufactured at Mallorytown, but several disinterested persons repeat this claim. Among these is Mrs. Erwin Mallory. She was told by her mother, Mrs. Ezechial Shipman, that a quilting party was held in the Burnham home in 1896, that the then Mrs. Burnham had laid a table made locally with a linen tablecloth woven by a Mrs. Burnham two generations removed, and that on the locally made table, on the locally made tablecloth, "rested the sugar bowl." This was related to the writer at his residence, The Old Stone House, on September 28, 1957, before witnesses by Mrs. Erwin Mallory (Emma Jane Shipman).

The *Burnham bowl* is made from an aquamarine-coloured bottle glass. It is 5¾" from the base to the top of the cover. The bowl proper is 3¾" in height, and 4" in diameter at its widest. The cover is dome-shaped, with a rounded finial bearing the scar of the pontil rod, and a folded rim which fits into the flared edges of the bowl. It was obtained from Mr. Cuthwin Burnham, R.R. No. 3, Mallorytown.

The second item added to the collection is the *Shipman vase* or bottle. This piece is a long, narrow, free blown bottle having an elongated flared neck. It was obtained from Mr. Walter Shipman, a descendant of a United Empire Loyalist family. It has been termed a vase because of the extreme length of the widely flared neck. It is quite possible that bottles of this general shape were a commercial product of the Mallorytown works, but if so the necks must have been slightly less flared and

---

*The importance of early Quebec silver may be studied in the work, *The Old Silver of Quebec* by the late Professor Ramsay Traquair, the merits of Krieghoff and Kane as painters in *Cornelius Krieghoff* by Marius Barbeau, and Paul Kane's *Wanderings of an Artist*.

No. 8. Burnham Bowl and Cover (green). Pitcher (light green). Vase or
bottle (light green). Flask (light green). Mallorytown
Glass Works, Mallorytown, Ontario.

somewhat shorter. This piece is 8¾″ in height, and the width at the
widest is 2″. (A somewhat similar bottle is listed among the collections
of the Montreal Museum of Fine Arts.)

The third specimen to join the collection is the *Guild tumbler*. This
is an especially well authenticated piece, and was obtained from a branch
of the Guild family closely related to Mr. Fred Guild of Mallorytown.
It is made from the typical aquamarine bottle glass, and is 3⅛″ in height,
with a diameter of 2¾″ at the top. It is of course free blown, and resembles the modern shot glass in form. Mr. Guild was quite helpful
in adding this item to the collection.

The *Bates pitcher* is of great importance to the student of Canadian
glass. It suggests what has since been proven that the many techniques
used in shaping glass must not be attributed to one section of North

America only.    As is well known, itinerant glass blowers wandered from place to place and country to country.    Is it not strange that this fact was never associated with glass-making in Canada?    Why should Canada be the one country thought to be incapable of appreciating or fostering the craft of glass-making?    It has now been established that Canadian glass houses employed glass blowers trained in Europe, England and the United States.    Is it likely that these artists in glass would forget or discard all their knowledge when arriving in Canada?    Many techniques attributed to a specific country have been proven to have been used centuries before in the same medium or in different mediums.    A classic instance of this is the supposition that the "trailed" handle is the exclusive product of glass houses in the United States.    The fact is that the technique of the trailed handle was used by Roman glass blowers.

This preamble is necessary in discussing the authentication of the *Bates pitcher*.    This piece answers the question as to whether or not Canadian glass blowers understood and used the trailed handle and the superimposed decoration known as lily-pad.    The trailed handle is, of course, a handle whose termination does not finish with its joining the body of the piece, but is continued in one or more semi-circular loopings. The so-called lily-pad consists of a superimposed gather of glass added to the bottom of the piece.    This is drawn up over the globular part of the body in evenly spaced narrowing columns terminating in more or less circular finials.    The whole, being made from glass in a workable state, is of course incorporated into the finished piece.

The use of a threaded neck also dates from Roman times, as early as A.D. 400.    The method used in threading was to take a thread or stringer of glass of uniform size and wind it about the neck of the piece being completed; when applied to the bottom of a specimen, threading was usually in the form of inverted V's.    The *Bates pitcher* illustrates the techniques of trailed handle, lily-pad decoration, and a threaded neck. It is decorated with seven of the lily-pads, and is 6½" in height.    The lily-pads contribute to its width of 5¼".    The neck has eleven circles of applied threading.    The handle of course is applied, and the pitcher rests on a slightly domed foot.

This piece was known to the writer for a number of years, but could not be acquired until it was offered in auction.    Incidentally, the house at which the auction was held was built for an uncle of the author by his grandfather.

The source of the *flask* in the Collection must remain anonymous. It was obtained in the Mallorytown area and is of undoubted authenticity. It is free blown of heavy metal, and is typical of the era in form and use. It is a whisky flask, and resembles the later "historical" flasks so widely used throughout the Americas.

No. 9. (*In background*) Flask, Tumbler, Vase.  Made at Mallorytown.  (*In foreground*)
Shards of Fire Pots; chunk of Raw Glass (deep aquamarine); and Shards of Glass;
all excavated at the site of the Mallorytown Glass House.

There remain the two additional authenticated specimens manufactured at this first of Canadian glass houses.  These are a sugar bowl
and cover listed as the *Pierce bowl* and a *doorstop-paperweight*.  Both
pieces are in the collection of the author.

The first, the *Pierce bowl*, is identical in all ways with the previously
mentioned *Burnham bowl*.  The second, although crude, is the only known
example of a *Mallorytown doorstop*.  It is 3⅜″ in diameter, and 1¼″ in
height.  It is flattened, rather than oval like later Canadian paperweights.
This specimen was so scarified that jeweller's rouge was used to remove
an opaque film from the upper surface.  This revealed a crudely incorporated decoration consisting of red, white and blue chips of glass,
quite similar to pieces attributed to the northern New York State glass
houses of Redwood and Redford.  Could it be that glass blowers from
Mallorytown migrated to these American glass houses?  Or is the reverse
possible?  The distance, as the crow flies, between Mallorytown and
these northern New York State factories is surprisingly short, and in
severe winters the St. Lawrence River has always been used as a highway.

This doorstop-paperweight was authenticated by a study of its metal and technique, by descriptions supplied by Mallorytown families of chunks of glass used as doorstops and by the verification of these chunks by Mrs. Kathleen Purvis.

Later descriptions of paperweights made in Canada and of their manufacture will explain how glass of a colour not found in the glass manufactured in Mallorytown came to be used in this as yet unique piece. Glass blowers took pride in their knowledge of the medium. and had their little secrets.

It is hoped that further investigation will reveal additional specimens produced at this glass house, and that an official marker will indicate the location of this first Canadian attempt to produce the first man-made material.

## 2. The Hamilton Glass Works, Hamilton (1865-1895)

ORIGINS OF The Hamilton Glass Works of Hamilton, Ontario, are somewhat difficult to trace. The reason is that there were two glass houses located in Hamilton from 1875 to 1895, and that both houses were absorbed by the Diamond Glass Company, which in turn was to become the Dominion Glass Company Limited.

As far as can be discovered by the study of directories, newspapers and other records, The Hamilton Glass Works was established in 1865 by Gatchell, Moore & Co. By the year 1869 this glass house had changed ownership, and the new management apparently employed its own mould makers. Advertisements appearing in a directory of that year include such statements as: "The Hamilton Glass Works manufactures all kinds of druggist's glassware;" "Private moulds of every description (are) made to order, and Other press work (is) made to order." The same publication, the *Canada Directory* for 1869, prints another advertisement by this house which states that it has glass blowers skilled as "Bottle Manufacturers," who could produce "Flint and Green Glassware."

Associated with the company were George Rutherford, J. Winer, Lyman Moore and L. H. Brooks. These executives were presumably the shareholders and mould designers, as the working glass blowers are to be found listed as such.

The glass blowers working for this Hamilton house in its early period of operation included several men who remained with it for many years. They were Joseph Charlton, Samuel Pancost, Peter Menard, David Reed, Francis Mitchell, James Stevenson, William Mitchell, John Voll and David Pancost.

The inclusion of such names in a work of this kind may seem unnecessary, but names supply leads to collectors that may result in the acquisition of authentic specimens. The greatest problem faced by any serious collector is that of authentication, and names may lead to contacts with the descendants of early artisans who can provide this.

Although a more or less accurate list of the dates of operation of The Hamilton Glass Works has been compiled, the products of this house remain somewhat of a mystery. An attempt to determine the types of "private moulds of every description" used by it has shown little result. Its site is now covered by modern buildings, and the one means of determining authenticity more certain than documentary proof—excavation—is no longer available.

We do know that the Hamilton works was equipped with two furnaces. One was what was termed a tank furnace, and the other a pot. According to elderly residents of Hamilton whose memories may be relied upon, the tank furnace was of the whale back type, and the glass batch melted in this furnace earned it the epithet of green house. The pot furnace—a furnace without a top—was known as the amber house.

This information suggests that in later years the Hamilton works limited its production to containers of various kinds. One type made there—an innovation used by many glass houses—was a bottle of large size apparently free blown but actually blown in a mould. This technique involved the use of a two-piece mould in which the glass blower twirled the gather of glass as it expanded by blowing. Thus the bottle did not have the usual seams or fins that indicate the use of moulds. Nor did these bottles, although seeming to be free blown have the scar showing the use of a punty or pontil rod. Numbers of these bottles are to be found in and around Hamilton, but their owners are loath to part with them.

A number of whimseys were produced by the Hamilton glass blowers. These special pieces included a great many solid glass canes, free blown cuspidors, and glass balls in some numbers.

As far as can be ascertained, the first monkey shop in Ontario operated in this glass works. A monkey shop consisted of three persons, a glass blower and two assistants who concentrated their efforts on containers used for condiments or drugs.

The documented dates of this glass house are as follows:

1865-1866 { Hamilton Glass Works (Gatchell, Moore & Co., proprietors), Hughson and Warren Streets.

1868-1869
1869        } Hamilton Glass Works, 309 Hughson Street N.
1871-1872

1872-1873 } Hamilton Glass Works (Geo. Rutherford & Co., proprietors).
1874        305 Hughson Street N.

1875        Hamilton Glass Works, 309 Hughson Street N.

1876-1877  Hamilton Glass Works (Rutherford & Co., proprietors), Cor. Hughson and Macaulay.

1878-1879  Hamilton Glass Works, L. H. Brooks, manager. Hughson Cor. Picton. (An advertisement gives the names J. Winer, Geo. Rutherford, L. Moore and L. H. Brooks.)

1879-1880  Hamilton Glass Works, Hughson Cor. Picton.

1880-1881  Hamilton Glass Works, Rutherford & Co., Hughson and Macaulay.

1881-1882⎫
1882-1883⎪
1883-1884⎬Hamilton Glass Works, L. H. Brooks, manager, 305 Hughson N.
1884-1885⎪
1885-1886⎭

1886-1887⎫Hamilton Glass Company, 309 Hughson.
1887-1888⎭

1888        Hamilton Glass Company, G. Rutherford, pres., Lyman Moore,
            vice-pres. and managing director, 295-313 Hughson N.

1888-1889⎫Hamilton Glass Company, 309 Hughson N.
1889-1890⎭

1890-1891⎫
1891-1892⎬Hamilton Glass Works, 439 Hughson N.
1892-1893⎭

1893-1894 Hamilton Glass Company—Diamond Glass Co., Ltd., James
          St. N.   Diamond Glass Co., Ltd. (Hamilton Glass Works),
          23 Picton E.

1894-1895 Diamond Glass Co., Ltd. (Hamilton Glass Works), H. H.
          Lloyd, mgr., 23 Picton E.

The greater part of the above information was supplied through the
splendid efforts of Dr. Freda Waldon, Chief Librarian, and Dorothy E.
Simpson, Head of the Reference Department, Hamilton Public Library.
In general, it may be accepted as authentic.   Although several editions
of *Canada Directories* differ somewhat, such differences are inconsequential.

This list indicates that this glass house, like The Burlington Glass
Works of Hamilton, was of prime importance to the history of Canadian
glass.   Throughout the years it employed many of the leading Canadian
glass experts.   Its glass blowers included many Canadian-trained men,
as well as immigrants from the United States and other countries.

The following is a list of glass blowers and workers employed by
the Hamilton Glass Works.   Notations indicate the directories in which
these names were found.   "H" indicates a directory published in Hamilton.
"T" a directory published in Toronto, "C" a *Canada Directory*; the
numbers show the year in which the directory was published.

George Anderson, blower, (H-97) (H-99)

Andrew Bard, blower, (H-89) (H-97)

George A. Bard, blower, (H-89) (T-97)

Thomas Bard, blower, (H-79) (H-95) (H-97) (H-99)

Charles Barnes, worker, (H-79)

Jeremiah Behan, blower, (H-89) (H-95) (T-97)

Charles Brown, blower (H-79)

Charles H. Brown, blower (H-79)

Joseph Brunt, blower, (H-79)

William Burnett, blower, (H-79)

Patrick Burns, blower, (H-89)

John Byrnes, blower, (H-97)

James Cahill, blower, (H-95)

Joseph Cahill, worker, (H-89)

Michael Cahill, blower, (H-79)

Joseph Charlton, blower, (C-65) (H-79) (H-89) (H-95) (H-97) (H-99)

Joseph Collins, blower, (H-89)

John E. Cook, blower, (H-95)

Michael Conway, blower, (H-89)

Matthew Cooper, blower (H-89)

Alfred Crist, blower (H-89)

Samuel Crist, blower, (H-79) (H-89) (H-95)

Ed. Cummerford, blower, (H-79) (H-95) (H-97) (H-99)

Samuel Dolman, blower, (H-89) (H-95) (T-97)

Matthew Doolan, blower, (H-97)

John Doolan, blower, (H-97)

John Doyle, worker, (H-89)

Wm. Dummer, blower, (H-89) (H-95)

Agustus Fickle, packer, (H-89)

George Foster, blower, (H-89)

John Griffin, blower, (H-95) (H-97)

Stephen Griffin, blower, (H-97) (H-99)

W. B. Griner, blower, (H-89) (T-97)

John Hafner, blower, (H-89) (H-95) (H-99)

Wm. Hagan, blower, (H-79)

Pat Halloran, blower, (H-89) (H-95) (H-97)

Charles Hanley, blower, (H-89)

James Harold, blower, (H-89)

John Harold, blower, (H-79) (H-95)

John Harrigan, blower, (H-79)

G. E. Harris, blower, (H-79) (H-95) (T-97)

James Harvey, blower, (H-79)

D. Husted, blower, (H-79)

James Jones, blower, (H-95)

Thomas Kellivan, blower, (H-79)

James Kenney, blower, (H-79)

Charles Knipe, blower, (H-95)

Thomas Lee, blower, (H-89)

Henry H. Lloyd, manager, (H-95) (Acct. Diamond Glass H-99)

R. McHenry, blower, (H-79)

Joseph McMann, blower, (H-89)

William McMann, blower, (H-89)

Thos. McNichol, blower, (H-95) (T-97)

Jos. McGuire, blower, (H-95)

Peter Menard, blower, (C-65) (H-79)

Henry Miller, blower, (H-79)

Francis Mitchell, blower, (C-65) (H-79)

Albert Mooney, blower, (H-79)

Arthur Murphy, blower, (H-79)

John Murphy, blower, (H-95) (H-99)

Cornelius Mynaham, sorter, (H-89)

James O'Donnah, blower, (H-79)

Stephen O'Donell, blower, (H-79) (H-89)

Michael O'Neil, blower, (H-79) (H-89) (H-95) (H-97) (H-99)

David Pancost, blower, (C-65)

Samuel Pancost, blower, (C-65)

Thos. Pearson, blower, (H-89) (H-95) (H-97) (H-99)

Rudolph Peters, blower, (H-95)

Harry Priestland, blower, (H-79)

Ed. Rawson, blower, (H-95) (H-97)

John Ray, blower, (H-97)

Daniel Reardon, blower, (H-97)

David Reed, blower, (C-65)

John Reid, blower, (H-79) (H-95)

Fred Riminn, blower, (H-89)

John Roach, worker, (H-95)

John Schiflee, blower, (H-79)

Thos. Sindell, blower, (H-79)

John Smith, blower, (H-79)

Stephen Summers, blower, (H-79)

James Stevenson, blower, (C-65)

Joseph Trapps, blower, (H-79)

John Voll, blower, (C-65) (H-79) (H-89)

One point revealed by this list should be noted. The glass blowers designated by the letters "C" and "T" were those masters of their trade who moved from glass house to glass house. It appears that the early (1865) workers were trained in the factories located in and about Montreal, and the later (T-97) glass blowers were chosen to go to the newer factories in Toronto and assist in training their men and increasing their output.

Personal interviews with surviving glass blowers have revealed that the Diamond Glass Company sent men from Hamilton to Toronto, Wallaceburg and Montreal. Further investigations have disclosed that several Hamilton trained men were employed in the glass houses of Nova Scotia.

The supposition that there was no nineteenth century Canadian glass can be refuted merely by reading the above list of names and dates. That number of glass blowers working for that number of years could produce many hundred of tons of glass, and this factory was but one of many.

### AUTHENTICATED SPECIMENS

Although authenticated products of The Hamilton Glass Works are somewhat rare, one piece exists which is unique so far as Canada is concerned. This item is merely a blown glass ball, but it is an integral part of a well documented Canadian legend, for it belonged to Mother Barnes, the Witch of Plum Hollow.

Canadian history makes little mention of witches that will withstand the hard light of research, but the story of Mother Barnes is still remembered in the county of Leeds, Ontario. Mrs. Barnes was not strictly speaking a witch, but a woman who with the aid of tea leaves foretold coming events, located misplaced or stolen articles, and on occasion made rather grim prognostications. Memory of her has been kept alive by articles in newspapers in Ottawa and Kingston by elderly persons who had visited her, and, most important of all, by two volumes written by a contemporary: *The Witch of Plum Hollow* by Thad. W. H. Leavitt (The Wells Publishing Company, Toronto, 1892) and a *History of Leeds and Grenville* by the same author (The Recorder Press, Brockville, Ontario, 1879). Both of these works stress the importance of Mother Barnes as an oracle, and tell of visitors from all parts of Canada and the United States making their way to her door on foot, on horseback and by hired buggy.

No. 10.   Free-blown Glass Ball.   Deep amber bottle glass.   Said to have been in the possession of Mrs. Barnes—the "Witch of Plum Hollow."
Free-blown cuspidor (Deep amber bottle glass), Hamilton Glass Works.   (*Circa 1885*).

Commercial Containers.   Hamilton Glass Works.   (*Circa* 1870-1890).

The authenticity of this *witch ball* may be questioned.   But anyone who has visited old manor houses or castles in England may remember seeing such glass *witch balls* suspended in windows.   They are mentioned, too, in *American Glass* by George and Helen McKearin (page 634). Their purpose was to keep unfriendly spirits from entering premises protected by their magical powers.   These *witch balls* were produced by glass houses in great numbers.

This specimen was obtained from Mrs. H. (Geraldine) Clark, through the efforts of Miss Harriet Robertson.  (Mrs. Clark was a noted collector, and was interested in the history of the county of Leeds.) The ball is blown from heavy metal, and is dark amber in colour—typical bottle glass.   It is 13½" in circumference, and has an opening measuring ½".   Glass balls of this type were reproduced at The Hamilton Glass Works.   Many were silvered on the inner side and used as the finials on lightning conductors.

Another Hamilton piece is a *cuspidor*.   Like the witch ball, it is merely a free blown glass ball.   The gather of glass was blown and expanded into a round glass ball, which was then pressed against the corner of, possibly, a marver.   The result was a ball flattened and depressed from both sides. the mouth of the cuspidor was the opening left by the removal of the blow pipe.   This was not a commercial product, but a piece made to be discarded when it had served its purpose; it could not be emptied.

This specimen measures 8¾" at its widest, and is 3⅞" in height. The metal is dark amber in colour.   It was obtained from the late Miss Christina McCaskill of Hamilton.   Miss McCaskill wrote that she had acquired this piece locally, and that it had been made by a man who "had worked in the Hamilton glass works, at the corner of James and Picton."   The item was cross-checked with residents of Hamilton familiar with the products of the house.

Several specimens of the commercial output of this house have been discovered. Among the oldest of these is a *bottle* embossed with the name "Pilgrim Bros & Co—Hamilton."   It bears the design of an eagle with wings extended standing on a ribbon.   The ribbon bears the words "trade mark."   The bottle is 10¾" in height, and 10½" in circumference. It was made from a heavy metal, coloured olive green in a two-piece mould.   The mould was apparently so well made that it left no mould marks.   This is a pecularity of moulds produced in the Hamilton works. The reason may have been that they were made from wood.   This is suggested by the great numbers of small rectangular marks suggesting chipping that may be seen on the bottle.

One of the standard products of the Hamilton works was a container of the sealer type; that is a *preserving jar*. Apparently these containers were made in several sizes; it has been established that quart and half-gallon jars were made in great numbers. The half-gallon ones were marked No. 4, and the quart size was embossed 1 quart. Both had the name of the company, Hamilton Glass Works, moulded into the glass.

Some account of how the sealers illustrated herein were acquired will show in what manner collectors gather their collections.

The collector from whom these examples were obtained writes:

I was driving through the countryside in the vicinity of Jordan, near Niagara Falls, when I came to a roadside stand at which an elderly lady offered home-made dill pickles for sale. Several of the jars in which the pickles were stored appeared to be of an early type. I stopped, studied her wares, and decided that I must own the jars (we made our own home-made dills!). We asked the lady if she had a clean washpan or something similar. She said she had, and went into her house. On her return with a large tin receptacle, we purchased three of the sealers, emptied the pickles into the pan, paid the lady in full, and drove away feeling that we had made a very good deal. We can still remember the puzzled look on the elderly lady's face. Apparently she had never encountered a collector before.

The first of the specimens acquired from this source is a half-gallon jar made from a glass which is a deep aquamarine in colour. It is 9½″ in height, and 14½″ in circumference. The second, the 1 quart, is 7¾″ in height, and 12¼″ in circumference, but the glass is much closer to a true flint. It is interesting to note that the half-gallon's lid, which is flat, has a distinct bluish colour, and bears the words "Hamilton Glass Works;" the lid of the quart sealer matches the body of the piece. Both covers are held on by iron clamps adjusted by a thumbscrew. Both pieces were made in four-piece moulds. These consisted of two sections extending up to the neck; from here to the flared rim two additional sections were used. The larger of the two, the half-gallon, has the chipping marks typical of this glass house.

A number of these containers have since been added to the collection. One of these, 8″ in height and complete with cover and clamp, is now in the Royal Ontario Museum. Additional specimens will be acquired.

Another Hamilton piece obtained by Miss McCaskill and authenticated by Mr. George Gardiner is a *free blown bottle* dating 1865-1875. This appears to have the vestige of a mould mark, but the mark is merely evidence that the bottle has been rolled on a marver. This bottle holds an

No. 11.   Free-blown Bottle: Olive green bottle glass.
Hamilton Glass Works.   (*Circa 1870*).

imperial gallon, and was made from a dark olive green glass. It is perfectly cylindrical for 8¼″, with a circumference of 20″. The sharply sloping shoulder and the elongated neck give it a total height of 16¾″. The lip is widely collared, and the kick-up and scar made by the punty are typical of a type of bottle soon to disappear from the commercial market. Although this container is contemporary with the Pilgrim bottle, the technique used in its making is a hold-over from much earlier times. The demand for narrow-necked glass containers had increased throughout the world, and a new technique for finishing the necks and mouths of bottles had been perfected. This method was achieved by use of a snap or snap case. This was a tool said to have been invented circa 1850, and the type used in the earlier years of operation of both the Hamilton and Burlington works consisted of a handle equipped with movable arms which could be adjusted by means of a clip or ring. These were used in making mould blown bottles and stemmed wares of many kinds. The use of a snap eliminated the punty; by 1900 this tool was used only to complete special orders and, of course, whimseys.

For a detailed and authoritative résumé of wine and spirit bottles, the reader is referred to *American Glass*, pages 423-430.

## 3. The Burlington Glass Works, Hamilton (1875-1909)

FROM THE viewpoint of the collector, The Burlington Glass Works, of Hamilton, Ontario, is the most interesting Canadian glass works. The reason is that research relative to this house is possible in directories, newspapers, and personal interviews with surviving members of the working staff. There sources may be cross-checked to some extent by shards obtainable on the site. This matter of sites and their availability is of the utmost importance, for apart from catalogues issued by a glass house the investigation of the site upon which it was located is the one source from which exact conclusions may be drawn. Newspapers, directories and other forms of documentation may be questioned, but excavated shards provide proof beyond doubt.

A researcher is indeed fortunate when a site is available. The rapid growth of cities and the Canadians' lack of interest in their past

No. 12.   Ruins of the Burlington Glass Works, Hamilton, Ontario.

have combined to make his task difficult by causing the evidence of past achievements to disappear.  Happily, this is not the case with The Burlington Glass Works.  A person may admire on one hand the sparkle of Burlington Bay and on the other the gleam of glass fragments manufactured during the nineteenth century.  He may discover the dates of this glass house in the Hamilton Public Library, have lunch at the Yacht Club, and stroll to the entrance of the Yacht Club grounds, where he will find the site occupied by The Burlington Glass Works during the nineteenth and early decades of the twentieth centuries.  All about him

are the evidences of a glass house.   A lone stump marks the spot where
the foundations of the sorting room was located.   Little remains, but that
little is most helpful to historians.   It is strange indeed, that this site
is not marked with an official plaque.

Although The Burlington Glass Works is of fairly recent date compared with glass houses in Europe, it operated at a time when the
techniques of glass manufacture had remained constant for over fifty
years.   Glass made here was shaped by blowpipe and punty, by blowing
it in a mould, by pressing or by casting, and was decorated by means of
acid, cutting, sandblasting and paint.   Special pieces were engraved
with the names of individuals.   During the period 1875-1915 glass-
makers used every technique but the pure mechanical, and The Burlington
Glass Works was no exception.

In this glass house were trained many of the artisans whose mastery
of the medium was transmitted to present day Canadian glass workers.
From Burlington blowers and finishers were sent to Toronto, Wallaceburg,
Montreal and the Maritimes.   During lay-offs many of them worked
in glass houses in the United States, bringing new techniques and moulds
on their return to Canada.

Although the existence of this Canadian glass house was well known
to many elderly residents of Hamilton, collectors and authorities at
home and abroad had either ignored its immense output or had been
unaware that such an establishment had existed.

The Burlington Glass Works employed several hundred men, and was
equipped with both a pot and a tank furnace.   The commercial output
included fruit jars, butter dishes, sugar bowls, fruit dishes with covers,
lamps, lamp shades, lamp chimneys, bird cups, revolver bottles, egg
cups, bottles up to five gallons and many special items made to order.
In milk glass (opal) they made salt and pepper shakers, Easter eggs,
lamps and lamp shades, dishes, bottles, table wares, pipes and many
other articles.   The colours of the glass ranged from clear (flint) through
every hue and tint to deep olive green, and in milk glass from milk white
to fiery opalescent, through pale blue, deep blue, to purple slag.   Indeed,
the Burlington works experimented in every known coloration of glass.
Some of the master craftsmen imported sticks of special glass for making

No. 13.  George Gardiner, 1904 (*left*).  William Godkin Beach, born in Athens, Ontario (*right*).

paperweights and other whimseys, at a cost of up to five dollars a pound. Colours included a deep ruby, a deep blue and an amber, the latter appearing as black.  They were used to provide the chips forming the coloured grounds in paperweights.

With the decline of its rival, The Hamilton Glass Works, the Burlington glass house may be considered to have become the most important glass works in Canada.  The period 1880-1910 was one of general progress; the Burlington house kept abreast of such innovations as gas street lights and domestic lamps burning coal oil or kerosene.  It introduced a technique of blowing street light globes in wooden moulds, bringing the cost of this form of lighting within the reach of smaller municipalities.

The intense interest shown by The Burlington Glass Works in lamps and lighting equipment is indicated by the following dates and names of management personnel.

1865-1866  Murray A. Kerr, Clerk mechanical depot G.W.R.
1868          Murray A. Kerr, Coal oil and lamps.
1869          Murray A. Kerr, wholesale and retail dealer in coal oil and lamps.
1870          Same as 1869.
1870-1875  During these years Mr. Kerr continued to be a wholesale and retail dealer in coal oil, lamps and trimmings.
1875-1876  Burlington Glass Works.  E. R. Kent & Co. prop. (first entry); M. A. Kerr, wholesale lamps.
1876-1877  Edward R. Kent, Burlington Glass Works; M. A. Kerr, wholesale lamps, etc.
1877-1878  Burlington Glass Co., cor. Burlington and McNab Streets; Edward R. Kent, commercial traveller (glass?); Murray A. Kerr, same.
1878-1879  Burlington Glass Co., M. A. Kerr, W. G. Beach.  (From this date Mr. Kent apparently terminates his association with this company.)
1879-1880  W. G. Beach, manager, Burlington Glass Works
1880-1881  W. G. Beach, Burlington Glass Works
1881-1882  Burlington Glass Works, M. A. Kerr, prop.; Wm. G. Beach, manager, Burlington Glass Works
1882-1883⎫
1883-1884⎬ Burlington Glass Co., Murray A. Kerr, prop.  W. G. Beach
1885-1886⎭ not listed after this date.)
1886-1887  Burlington Glass Co., Murray A. Kerr, Lyman Moore, George Rutherford (see Hamilton Glass Co.)
1887-1888  Burlington Glass Works
1888-1889⎫
1889-1890⎬ Burlington Glass Works, cor. Burlington and MacNab
1890-1891  Lyman Moore, Burlington Glass Works
1891-1909  The Burlington Glass Works remains listed as at Burlington and MacNab Streets.  After 1910 the Glass Works is not listed.

When doing research on the glass houses of Hamilton one encounters repeated listings of a "Canada Glass House, H. Kent, prop."  It is possible that this establishment was a retail and wholesale outlet for The Burlington Glass Works during the regime of Edward R. Kent, but it did not manufacture glass.

Another point worthy of note is that during the latter part of its existence The Burlington Glass Works was under the ownership of the Diamond Glass Company.  This was learned orally, not from directories.

An excerpt from *The Year Book and Almanac of Canada for 1876; being an Annual Statistical Abstract of the Dominion* gives an indication of the production for that year in Canadian glass houses, including those of Hamilton. Page 24, under the heading "The Census of Canada," lists: "Glass works, 6; Hands Employed: Male, 309; Female, ——. Yearly Wages, $104,800; Value of Raw Material, $102,275; Value of Articles Produced, $293,130."

Taking into account the purchasing power of the dollar in 1876, a production at over a quarter of a million dollars is presumptive proof that much of the early glass still to be found in Canada was produced in this country. The need for domestic manufacture is found in the high customs duties on imported wares. As late as 1891 the Canadian tariff was imposing a duty of 30 per cent on imported glass carboys and demi-johns, bottles and decanters, flasks and phials, telegraph and lightning rod insulators, jars and glass balls, and cut, pressed or moulded table wares. Charged at other rates were lamp and gas-light shades, lamps and lamp chimneys, globes for lanterns, lamps, etc., glass stained, tinted or painted, figured, enamelled and obscured white glass, and glass made into pendants, window glass, or silvered.

One may deduce from the figures supplied by the *Year Book* of 1876 that in that year alone Canadian glass blowers supplied the home market with approximately a million items of glass. To support these statistics, we append a documented list of glass workers employed in The Burlington Glass works, and arranged alphabetically, obtained from Hamilton directories (H) of the dates shown, and in one case from a Toronto directory (T).

B. Anderson, worker, (H-79) (H-89)
J. Anderson, worker, (H-79)
John Berlinghoff, blower, (H-79)
E. H. Bowen, blower, (H-79)
Patrick Burke, blower, (H-97)
John Burnes, blower, (H-79)
M. Burnes, blower, (H-79)
J. Campbell, worker, (H-79) (H-95)
E. Conley, worker, (H-79)
Michael Conway, blower, (H-79)
Eugene Crist, blower, (H-79)

Edward Daly, blower, (H-97) (H-99)
Wm. Dillon, worker, (H-79) (H-99)
Robert Dillon, blower, (H-95)
Robert Douglas, blower, (H-89) (H-95) (H-97)
John Dunn, blower, (H-89)
R. Earl, worker, (H-79)
Wm. Earl, worker, (H-79)
A. Foralinger, blower, (H-79)
J. Ford, worker, (H-79)
Jas. Fritman, blower, (H-89)

Charles Furlong, blower, (H-79) (H-95) (H-97) (H-99)
Daniel Furlong, blower, (H-95) (H-97) (H-99)
Moses Furlong, blower, (H-79) (H-95) (H-97) (H-99)
George Gardiner, blower, (H-86) (H-90) (H-95) (H-99)
Joseph Gormley, blower, (H-79) (H-89) (H-95)
John Gray, blower, (H-99)
Robert Gray, blower, (H-79) (H-89) (H-95) (H-97) (H-99)
T. Gray, blower, (H-79)
Wm. Gray, blower, (H-79) (H-95) (H-97) (H-99)
Robert Gray, blower, (H-97)
Geo. Haves, blower, (H-95)
Thos. Haves, blower, (H-95) (H-99)
Wm. Haves, blower, (H-95)
Leonard Herr, blower, (H-95)
Wm. Hogan, blower, (H-79)
John Hunter, blower, (H-79)
Wm. Hunter, blower, (H-79)
Daniel Husted, blower, (H-89)
Thomas Jones, blower, (H-79) (H-89) (H-97) (M-71)
J. Jordan, blower, (H-79)
E. Kelly, blower, (H-79)
Lawrence Kelly, blower, (H-97) (H-99)
L. Kelly, Jr., blower, (H-97)
A. Kennedy, blower, (H-79)
Thomas Kenney, blower, (H-89)
Ralph King, manager, (H-95) (H-97)
H. McCloy, blower, (H-79)
Thomas McCloy, blower, (H-79)
William McGinnis, blower and finisher, (H-79) (H-80) (H-85) (H-90) (H-97)
James McMahon, blower, (H-79)
Joseph McMahon, blower, (H-79)
Charles McNichol, blower, (H-79) (H-89) (H-95) (H-97) (T-98)
John McNichol, blower, (H-89) (H-97) (T-98)
-. McGrady, worker, (H-79)
J. Mahoney, blower, (H-79)
N. Mahoney, blower, (H-79)
J. C. Malcolmson, foreman, (H-89) (T-97)
H. H. Malcolmson, blower, (H-97) (T-98)

Geo. F. Miles, blower, (H-89)
J. Mooney, worker, (H-79)
C. Moynihan, blower, (H-79) (H-99)
James Munam, worker, (H-79)
George Mullin, blower and finisher, (H-79) (H-99)
R. Mullin, worker, (H-79)
John Murphy, blower, (H-97)
Jos. Murphy, blower, (H-89) (H-95) (H-99)
Pat Murphy, blower, (H-79)
T. Murphy, blower, (H-99) (T-97)
James Noble, blower, (H-79)
Martin Nolan, blower, (H-89) (H-95) (T-97)
A. O'Brien, worker, (H-79)
Thos. O'Connor, worker, (H-79)
James O'Donnell, blower, (H-79) (H-89) (H-95) (H-97) (H-99)
Bernard O'Neil, blower, (H-97)
Jno. C. O'Neill, worker, (H-79) (H-97) (H-99)
Thos. O'Neill, blower, (H-97)
J. Parks, worker, (H-79)
Ed. Phillips, blower, (H-90) (H-95) (H-97) (T-98)
Jos. Phillips, worker, (H-79) (H-97)
John Phillips, Jr., blower, (H-97)
Robt. Phillips, blower, (H-97)
Wm. Reid, blower, (H-89)
Ed. Roach, blower, (H-97) (H-99)
R. Roach, blower, (H-79) (H-89) (H-95)
Peter Shaw, mould maker, (H-89)
F. Smith, worker, (H-79) (H-97) (H-99)
Samuel Smith blower, (H-89) (H-95) (H-97) (H-99)
Stephen Smith, blower, (H-95) (H-97) (H-99)
Patrick Wickham, blower, (H-95) (T-97) (M-97) (M-98) (H-99)
James Welsh, worker, (H-79)
James Whittaker, blower, (H-79) (H-99)
-. Whittaker, blower, (H-99)
-. Whittaker, blower, (H-99)
W. Wilkinson, worker, (H-79)
Richard Williams, blower, (H-97) (H-99)
Richard Williams, blower, (H-97)
Richard Williams, Jr., blower, (H-97)
Richard Witt, blower, (H-89) (H-97)

Some of the glass blowers listed as working at the Burlington works were among the most skilled practitioners of their craft. These men either developed techniques new to Canada or taught younger craftsmen the existing methods of producing such difficult pieces as paperweights. Although blown and manipulated weights were made in Canada until a comparatively late date, it appears that these were never considered a commercial article. As far as has been established, the better types of weights were made only for presentation purposes, or as proof of a glass blower's proficiency in the medium.

Although a number of glass paperweights have been traced to individual glass blowers, several authenticated weights are so far only traceable to the glass house in which they were made. The most important of the known paperweight makers (all of Burlington) were: William McGinnis, George Mullin, Patrick Wickham, George Gardiner, Edward (Nix) Daly, James O'Donnell, Charles McNichol and Patrick Murphy.

According to oral reports, the most outstanding of these men were William (Billy) McGinnis and George Mullin. Their names occur in the above documented list of glass blowers as "blower and finisher."

A few private individuals scattered throughout Canada had known for some time that many types of glass were formerly made in Hamilton, but this did not become public knowledge until, following an advertisement in the Hamilton *Spectator*, one of the few surviving nineteenth century Canadian glass blowers was located. This was Mr. George Gardiner, who had begun his apprenticeship with The Burlington Glass Company in 1885. Mr. Gardiner was most helpful, and was pleased that the old days were of interest.

A general knowledge of glass-making may be obtained from text books, but the unofficial terminologies and techniques in use in glass factories can be learned only from one who has worked at the craft. It is thus that tricks of the trade and personalities become known to researchers. Mr. Gardiner was indeed a find.

Interviews with Mr. Gardiner provided a great deal of information, which was inscribed in notebooks and preserved by tape recorder. We were also taken over the site of the Burlington glass house, and presented with many shards of glass picked up by Mr. Gardiner on his daily stroll past the old works.

When making a study of this kind it is well to call in question any source until it has been proven reliable by cross-checking. We therefore cross-checked the names, dates and other data supplied us by Mr. Gardiner. Everything was confirmed. Names of persons and factories were found listed in directories, and at the proper dates and locations. Thanks to this combination of sources, and the availability of the site, we found that many types of glass could be credited to the Burlington glass house.

Interesting sidelights on glass-making and the personalities of glass blowers of the late nineteen hundreds were provided by Mr. Gardiner. Although glass blowers were the aristocracy of labour and received a very high rate of pay, they were not as unthrifty as has been suggested. Their one vice was gambling. According to Mr. Gardiner they would "make a bet on anything from a cockfight to the number and size of bottles blown in a day." They were a closely-knit fraternity, and formed their own baseball and hockey teams, choirs and orchestras. When feeling pugnacious, as happens quite often during parades or "walks," they always picked on innocent bystanders of other trades. They were great fishermen. Living as they did in close proximity to Burlington Bay, the long summer lay-off—usually one and a half to two months—allowed them time to indulge in this pastime. The long holiday was made necessary by the heat of July and August, when working conditions became unbearable.

When a glass blower learned that an important horse race was to take place, he could wangle a day off by "slipping an iron" or "dropping the pig." Either of these "accidents" caused the batch to turn green, and also made it almost impossible to collect a gather on the blowpipe. (An iron was of course a blowpipe, and a pig was a rest in the mouth of the furnace upon which a blow pipe could be rolled.

Mr. Gardiner corrected misconceptions about several loosely used glass house terms. He explained that "end-of-day" glass was a mis-nomer in the case of the Burlington glass house, since the factory worked on twenty-four hour shifts, and such whimseys as were made by the glass blowers were produced during their lunch hour; a new shift would not approve of a worker staying over "and cluttering up the place." He explained that "flint" glass was merely a trade name; that only occasionally, when a special order was received, did the Burlington house produce lead glass; and that the general output was of the cheaper variety—lime glass—introduced during the 1860's.

Mr. Gardiner also stated that glass blowers were sometimes lent to other glass houses, both in the United States and Canada. This would happen when there was a breakdown at a factory, or when a special rush order had been received. These breakdowns had various causes: trouble with a furnace, bad batches, and that curse of early glass houses, fire. Mr. Gardiner told of an interruption of work at The Hamilton Glass Works when, in some manner the tank furnace developed a great crack in the wall and the molten glass flowed out of the glass works and across the street before it cooled sufficiently to harden. This happened when he was a small boy, and he recalls that it was spoken of as resembling the eruption of a volcano.

Mr. Gardiner's statement about the exchange of personnel between glass houses is important, and accounts for the similarity of techniques in different glass houses sometimes encountered by the researcher. This Canadian glass blower blew glass in Hamilton, Toronto and Wallaceburg in Canada, and in Milwaukee, Terre Haute and Chicago in the United States.

Mr. Gardiner opened the door to many discoveries, the most important of which was that certain types of glass paperweights could be credited to Canadian glass blowers. We were to discover later that this had been known to several executives of the Dominion Glass Company, but to us and to the Canadian public the fact that glass paperweights had been manufactured in nineteenth century Ontario and Quebec glass houses came as a very pleasant surprise.

Mr. Gardiner was able to produce two paperweights of his own making and another made for and given to Mrs. Gardiner by Patrick (Pat) Wickham. Mr. Wickham cannot be classed as an outstanding exponent of this particular art, as his weights were invariably made from bottle glass of a dark aquamarine colour with a simple white field of opal glass upon which is written in pencil the name of the person for whom the weight was made.    Mr. Wickham's importance lies in the fact that he worked in glass houses associated with the Diamond Glass Company in Hamilton, Toronto and Montreal.

If it had not been for Mr. Gardiner, the many examples of the work of Pat Wickham that turn up from time to time could not have been authenticated.    Apparently Mr. Wickham was the most prolific of the Canadian paperweight makers, but one of the most interesting examples of his work is that obtained from Mr. Gardiner.    This deep aquamarine bottle glass weight inscribed "Della Hollyman" is truly an important piece of Canadiana.    Although crude in technique, when compared to the splendid examples produced in France, the authentic story associated with this piece makes it unique.    This weight was made, as is shown by the date (1898), by Pat Wickham in the Toronto Glass Works (see chapter 5).    It was made to the order of Ed Phillips (the initials E.P. are to be seen on the upper right corner of the white field), and was presented to Miss Della Hollyman, 1898, on the occasion when she acted as bridesmaid at her sister's marriage to Mr. Phillips.    Mr. Phillips, a glass blower at the Burlington works, had asked our informant, Mr. George Gardiner, to be his best man.    In this manner Mr. Gardiner and Miss Hollyman were introduced, and Miss Hollyman later became Mrs. Gardiner.    This is a well authenticated specimen, which enables a collector to authenticate other specimens of this glass blower's works.    All weights produced by Mr. Wickham were slightly flattened but circular in shape, and usually showed traces of some attempt to grind out the scar made by a pontil rod.

The glass paperweights made by Mr. Gardiner were, from a technical standpoint, much more advanced.    According to Mr. Gardiner, these weights were made under the direction of Billy McGinnis.    Mr. McGinnis was the acknowledged master of his day in Canada, and instructed those glass blowers who were interested in learning the technique of paperweight making.    Mr. Gardiner stated, "Billy stood at my shoulder when I made my weights," and added, "Billy taught many blowers how to make weights, *canes, hats* and *drapes*."    The drapes were a product of the late Victorian period of florid decoration.    The known makers of such whimseys include George Gardiner, Billy McGinnis and James Canty.

No. 14. Drape ("candy-cane" triangular pieces; chain links of clear, milky, amber, violet, aubergine, blue and green glass ). Burlington Glass Works.

The *drapes* made by Mr. Gardiner are composed of a series of glass ornaments held together by chains, the links of which are formed from glass manufactured by the Burlington glass house. These are the most decorative of any so far authenticated, and consist of heart-shaped ornaments of a candy-cane type connected by links. The one surviving drape made by Mr. Gardiner is now in the Edith Chown Pierce and Gerald Stevens Collection in the Royal Ontario Museum.

Billy McGinnis is said to have learned his trade in Canada. If this is so, and he is not to be found listed as having worked at the earlier Hamilton works, it is possible that he was apprenticed in one of the several glass houses in Montreal or its environs, in that of St. Johns, Quebec or in one of the Vaudreuil (Hudson) companies. We first learned about Mr. McGinnis from Mr. Gardiner. It appears that Billy could "make anything from glass," and several of his glass paperweights have been discovered. These have been authenticated by Mr. Gardiner, and the similarity of technique is obvious.

Although paperweights are the only examples of Billy's work so far discovered, it is doubtful that other examples of his whimseys will be authenticated. The reason is that *canes, hatchets*, etc., found in and about Hamilton could be the products of one or more of this master's pupils. Apparently each expert glass blower used distinctive techniques and passed them along to friends. Thus Mr. McGinnis made a lily type of paperweight, as did Mr. Gardiner. Of course there are differences, and in the case of Mr. Gardiner we know that his output was limited to two weights, but we have not learned of other specimens made under the tutelage of Billy McGinnis. This point is stressed because it concerns a type of weight made by another Canadian glass blower. Great numbers of lily weights were manufactured in the United States during the latter part of the nineteenth century.

Mr. George Mullin appears to have been the one Burlington glass blower whose production of whimseys was more varied than that of Mr. McGinnis. Mr. Mullin specialized in paperweights, hollow-blown pieces which he coated on the inner side with "mercury" and what is termed overlay glass. Mr. Mullin worked in many glass houses in Canada, including the Burlington Works, the Toronto Glass Works, and the Sydenham glass house in Wallaceburg.

The one type of paperweight authenticated as the work of Mullin is a clear glass weight encasing four domed mushroom-like mounds of coloured chips over which is suspended a strip of opal glass bearing a name. It is possible that Mr. Mullin made weights of other types, but if so we do not know of them. It was in Wallaceburg that the information about

Mr. Mullin's teaching other glass blowers the art of paperweight making was confirmed.

Mr. Mullin's method of making a glass cane revealed a nicety of technique not often encountered. This consisted of blowing and working a gather of glass until it resembled a modern bandmaster's baton, quite bulbous in the handle. Incorporated in the slightly twisted body of the piece were strips of glass coloured red, white and blue. When the piece had assumed its final shape, and before the tip was twisted and closed, the inside was silvered. The finished article was most decorative, and was in great demand. Mr. Mullin instructed a number of brother glass blowers, including Mr. Gardiner, in the techniques of making these canes, but their fragility was such that only one example of those manufactured at Burlington is known to survive.

Mr. Mullin's pieces also included great numbers of *glass hats* some of which are said to have been large enough to wear. One of the smaller type was discovered and shown to Mr. Gardiner. It was most interesting to watch the movements of Mr. Gardiner's hands when he was asked to demonstrate the methods used to make a hat from glass. He explained and re-enacted every move made by "George": how a small gather of glass was taken on a blow pipe, expanded by blowing, attached to a pontil rod (Mr. Gardiner said "punty"), detached from the blow pipe, cut open by means of a shears, worked and shaped until it was drawn out and given a widely flared lip, which was rolled back on two sides to form a western-type hat.

The *cuspidors* or spittoons blown by George Mullin have been described but not viewed. These were apparently made from either flint or green bottle glass and coated with opal (milk glass). In making these Mr. Mullin took full advantage of the equipment available in the Burlington works, using the cutting and polishing wheels to cut designs through the outer covering and thus obtaining the effect usually encountered in this type of glass.

The Burlington Glass Works were, for their day, quite advanced in the types of glass manufactured and the methods used to embellish and decorate special pieces. From specimens authenticated as having been produced by this house, it may be accepted that they used engraving, cutting and polishing wheels, acid "frosting", painting, enamelling and sandblasting to add sales appeal.

The sandblasting process is described in encyclopedias as "inviting a current of air or steam carrying sand at high velocity, used in etching glass." The Burlington works used steam, and it is possible that a great deal of glass listed as frosted was etched in this manner. According to Mr. Gardiner—and specimens examined—the men employed as sand-blasters at Burlington were very adept at adjusting the equipment so that fine and/or coarse sand at varying degrees of heat could be used. To achieve a fast inexpensive effect resembling cut glass designs without having to use the costly cutting and polishing wheels, the sandblasters would design tin stencils of various forms and use these to protect a given area from the sand blast. In this manner designs in solid tin of flags, flowers or names were fastened to a piece, and the piece was then sand-blasted and rendered opaque except for the designs which remained clear. Favourite forms included crossed Union Jacks and bunches of grapes. It appears that *lamp chimneys* and *pitchers* were the principal items decorated in this manner, besides the round, oval and rectangular cast paperweights which were the only type of paperweight that may be listed as a commercial product of this and other Canadian glass houses. In the case of paperweights the process was sometimes reversed.

## Authenticated Specimens

Paperweights:

A *glass paperweight* made by George Gardiner, 1898. The body is of clear glass approximately 3″ in height with a circumference of 10¼″. This dome-shaped piece encloses a five petalled lily made from glass of a mustard colour, growing out of a ground consisting of multi-coloured chips of glass of variegated sizes. Many of these chips are larger than those usually found in Canadian weights, and appear to measure up to ¼″.

Another *glass paperweight* made by George Gardiner, 1898. This weight is similar in every respect to the preceding item with one exception: the lily was made from milk glass cased in greenish bottle glass, giving each petal the appearance of being broadly stripped. Both of the Gardiner weights reveal the use of a somewhat heavy pontil rod.

No. 15.   Paperweight made by George Gardiner in 1898.   Free-blown Hat made by George
Mullin, *(Circa 1885)*.   Paperweight made by William (Billy) McGinnis, *(Circa 1890)*.
Paperweight made by George Mullin, *(Circa 1890)*.   Free-blown Ball (Witch Ball?), light
amber.   Paperweight made by George Mullin, *(Circa 1895)*.
All products of the Burlington Glass Works.

A most interesting and historically important *glass paperweight* made *circa* 1885 by William (Billy) McGinnis. The clear glass body is approximately 2⅝″ in height, and 11″ in circumference. It is more rounded than domed, and is of the lily type. The white petals are attached to the usual bubble stem, and the ground is of finely chipped multi-coloured glass. It differs from the lily weights made by his pupil, Mr. Gardiner, in that the name of the person for whom it was made is included, a usual feature in Canadian paperweights. In the case of this weight the names—J. A. Johnson from Ettie Harris— were printed in cobalt on two narrow strips of opal glass, and these strips were incorporated into the weight between the petals of the lily and the coloured ground.* This weight has a story attached to the names. It has been learned that Johnson and Harris were bottle blowers capable of blowing containers of the largest sizes: i.e. men of great lung capacity. The combined names could have been attached for a reason similar to that given in connection with the Della Hollyman weight mentioned in the text.

A *glass paperweight* approximately 2⅝″ in height, and 11″ in circumference. This is a typical McGinnis lily weight. The clear glass body incorporates a five-petalled lily whose lemon yellow petals are joined to a centre and stem made from a bubble resembling an elongated teardrop. The ground consists of the usual multicoloured chips heated to such a degree that they almost flow together. Midway between the ground and the petals are three strips of opal glass forming a triangle. On these strips, in cobalt, is the name C. E. Chapman, Montreal. Although this name has not been found associated with the Burlington glass house, that invariably reliable source, Mr. Gardiner, stated that "a Chapman was a traveller for the old works." If this is so, the weight could have been made for either the salesman or one of his family.

A *glass paperweight* made for Martin Kerr by William McGinnis. This weight too, could have some importance as a piece of Canadiana, as a Murray A. Kerr was on the executive of both the Hamilton and Burlington glass works. This piece exemplifies a most important technique invariably employed in the manufacture of paperweights by Mr. McGinnis. This is an arrangement of the coloured chips on the ground to form a many-pointed star. The number of points may vary, but the apparently haphazard placing of the chips *always* resulted in this star. Another means of authenticating a McGinnis weight is by the manner of placing the names contained in his weights. This is not a lily weight, but a clear glass example, quite rounded in form, having a single strip of milk glass upon which is printed the name. The strip floats midway between the

*A blue colour is imparted to potash glass by the addition of a little cobalt salt.

crown of the piece and the coloured ground. The weight is $2\frac{3}{8}''$ in height, and $9\frac{3}{4}''$ in circumference. The scar left by the use of a punty is, as in all weights manufactured by McGinnis, quite apparent and indicative of a punty $\frac{1}{2}''$ or less in diameter.

A *glass paperweight* made by Billy McGinnis from a clear non-lead glass. It is quite rounded in form and is $2\frac{1}{4}''$ in height and $9\frac{3}{4}''$ in circumference. This weight is as yet unique. It is possible that the future will reveal many glass paperweights made in Canada containing a ceramic decorative addition, but this is still the only authenticated weight of its type known to exist. This weight was made for P. B. Fetterly, London, Ontario. This in itself intrigued the writer, since his wife was Edith Fetterly, and there was an uncle in the family with the initials P. B. This weight has the name printed in blue on one strip of milk white glass and the city and province on another, the strips forming a V. The ceramic decoration, a bird in flight, is suspended midway between the multi-coloured ground and the name. The bird appears to be a commercial piece made for this particular purpose. The extended wings are blue, the head and tail green and the body brown; the neck has a white ring. Mr. McGinnis was noted for importing sticks of coloured glass from which to break chips, and various novelties such as this ceramic bird. In this manner colours and ornaments not native to a specific glass house were adopted by glass blowers, and used and passed along.*

A *glass paperweight* made by George Mullin, *circa* 1895. This is one of the most important pieces of Canadiana produced in this medium. It has a clear glass body in which is a milk glass strip bearing the words "Jno. B. Watt." This strip is suspended above a coloured base typical of the work of Mr. Mullin. As in most paperweights made from glass, the magnification resulting from the rounding clear glass body is such that the four mushroom-like mounds appear to be distributed throughout the total circumference. When the weight is reversed, the actual proportions are revealed, and it is discovered that the coloured ground measures only $2\frac{1}{8}''$, whereas the weight has a diameter of $3\frac{1}{8}''$. Such specimens of Mr. Mullin's work as have been discovered show a slight depression in the base allowing the scar of the punty to remain as evidence that these pieces were hand worked. The diameters of these scars vary between $\frac{1}{2}''$ and $\frac{5}{8}''$. The height of this weight is $2\frac{3}{8}''$.

According to several Ontario and Canadian directories published during the last decade of the nineteenth century, John Watt was associated in an executive capacity with several Canadian glass houses located in Toronto and Hamilton. The Toronto directory of 1897 lists him as

---

*Additional paperweights attributed to and/or authenticated as being the work of William McGinnis are listed in the appendix among pieces of Canadian glass forming The Edith Chown Pierce and Gerald Stevens Collection in the Royal Ontario Museum.

president of the Toronto Glass Works, with residence in Hamilton.    We
have not the dates of Mr. Watt's first association with Canadian glass,
but we have the glass paperweight made for him by George Mullin.    Mr.
Gardiner remembers a Mr. Watt, but cannot recall the circumstances
other than that Watt was "a glass man."    The Hamilton Public Library
has made prolonged attempts to ascertain whether Mr. Watt's middle
initial was B.    According to Dr. Waldon, Chief Librarian, and Miss
Simpson, head of the reference department, Mr. Watt did not list a name
other than "Jno. Watt" or "John Watt" as identification.

Another *glass paperweight* made by Mr. Mullin is unique up to the
present time.    One of the coloured pieces forming one of the four mounds
is quite large in size and opaque white in colour.    On this in a very
small hand are the letters "G.M." in black.    According to Mr. Gardiner,
Mr. Mullin often signed special pieces, and his statement is confirmed
by this piece.    It is typical of this glass blower's technique, and is $2\frac{1}{2}''$
in height with a circumference of $10\frac{1}{2}''$.    Although the name of the person
for whom this piece was made has not been found listed in directories—
some dates are missing—a Mrs. Edward Lafferty is listed in the Hamilton
directory of 1897-1898, and Mr. George Gardiner claimed that he had
worked with an "Ed" Lafferty in the Burlington glass works.    Whether
or not this is the same man, this piece was made for E. Lafferty.    Another
characteristic technique employed by Mr. Mullin allows a cross-check of
weights attributed to his hand.    In both the Watt and Lafferty weights
is a small design drawn on both ends of each strip of the opal glass bearing
the names.    These marks resemble V's drawn at right angles.

The importance of these personal, non-commercial weights is
emphasized by an excerpt from *Old Glass Paperweights*, by Evangeline H.
Bergstrom, privately printed by The Lakeside Press, Chicago, 1940.
This authoritative work (now reprinted) states: "They [glass paperweights]
were frequently made for merchants and signed with the merchant's
monograms.    Such a signature indicates a good manufacturer."

It is the opinion of this writer that *any* manipulated glass paperweight, crude though it may be, is an object of some historical and cultural
importance, providing of course it is not of modern manufacture.    It
has been stated that frosted bases are modern.    Modern in what sense?
It has recently been established that commercial cast glass weights were
made in Hamilton glass houses from 1880 to 1905, and by Toronto glass
companies from 1894 to 1900, and that these cast weights were often
sandblasted on the bases so as to appear frosted.    Several nineteenth
century weights are also known to have bases finished off on grinding
wheels.    Can a date be set after which a weight could be declared
modern?

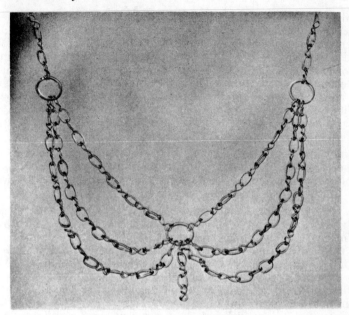

No. 16. Flint glass drape of the whimsey type.
Hamilton Glass Works, (*Circa 1885*).

## Other Special Pieces

A *glass drape* composed of four glass ornaments linked together by glass chains, the links being made both from imported glass and from batches manufactured in the Burlington works. The imported colours are few and consist mainly of a very deep ruby seldom made in this glass house. Although somewhat similar drapes were produced in many countries, these were a specialty of Canadian factories in Hamilton and Toronto in Ontario, and in the Maritimes. This particular piece was made by George Gardiner, *circa* 1895. It is 72″ in length, and the links composing the double chains average 1¾″. Each alternate link is of a clear glass joined to a coloured link, and the colours include amethyst, light, medium and dark blues, light and dark greens (some of these are bottle glass), light and dark amber (bottle glass), opal, custard and pale pinks. The techniques used in making the links were as varied as the colours, including solid glass, hollow links, cased glass and several variants.

According to Mr. Gardiner the cased links were made by gathering a stringer (a thin round piece drawn out to some length), working it, dipping it when ready into a batch of another colour, watching it until it almost melted and, just before it did, removing it to be stretched again into the desired length and diameter. Glass is one of the few media that allow such techniques to be used. The ornaments suggest a heart design, and are of a type known as candy glass. This consists of thin ribbons of red, white and blue encased in clear glass, then drawn out and twisted during the drawing.

A similar *glass drape* made by Mr. Gardiner. Sad to relate, this important piece of Canadiana is now in several pieces due to years of use, and the fact that a craftsman never values his own handiwork as much as that of someone else. Several of the ornaments from this piece are in the Edith Chown Pierce and Gerald Stevens Collection.

A clear *glass drape* with an overall length of 103″, made by joining three glass rings with a double glass chain the links of which average 2⅛″ in length. The glass rings at either end measure 3″ in diameter, while the central ring measures 4″. This drape is said to have been displayed above a bar in a now defunct hotel in Hamilton. As each ring is supplied with one loose link it appears that this decoration could have been fastened by means of these extra links. It is made from a very brilliant non-lead glass, and all links and rings were twisted in the making. The joints of all pieces, although very apparent, are carefully made and it is possible that this is a semi-commercial product.

A *glass hat* made by George Mullin in the Burlington works. This interesting specimen is the piece authenticated and described by Mr. Gardiner. It is made from a clear glass (flint) apparently similar to that used by this glass house to produce the more common types of chimneys for lamps. Its overall height is 2⅛″ the crown is 2¾″ in height and 2″ in diameter and the folded brim is 5⅛″ in length and 3¾″ at the narrowest point. The crown carries the scar of a bottle-blower's punty almost 1″ in diameter.

A blown *glass witch ball* was certainly manufactured from a commercial batch of light amber bottle glass made by the ton at the Burlington glass house. It is known that vast numbers of glass balls were made in this glass house for the purpose of decorating the early lightning-rods, particularly those on barns. The commercial product was silvered on the inner side, but the off-hand specimens were made from glass of all descriptions, and by every method known to the Burlington glass blowers. Indeed, this writer has been informed that small-sized glass balls were made for children, and that these as well as the ends removed from blown chimneys (see shards) were called snappers. When thrown, these snappers exploded with a distinct "pop."

The full story of hollow glass balls has yet to be written. Tradition credits the first use of "witch balls" to English glass blowers who, during the last decades of the eighteenth century, were a superstitious class. Authorities on this subject claim that the first specimens were made with a hole in which a string could be fastened. Balls made from glass blue in colour were said to have a therapeutic value over and above that of keeping witches away. Other writers suggest that a glass ball was the easiest means of making a reasonably airtight cover for glass containers. It is a well known fact that glass balls were and are used as floats for fishing nets, but the amber glass ball made in the Burlington works was certainly never used as a float, as it has an opening ¾″ in diameter. It is 13¾″ in circumference.

A *glass cane* made by George Mullin, *circa* 1895. This splendid example of a "bandmaster" cane was presented to The Edith Chown Pierce and Gerald Stevens Collection by Mr. Louis N. Long of Hamilton. (Mr. Long is a well-known maker of clay pigeons used in trap and skeet shooting.) This cane was given to Mr. Long by one of his school teachers, who taught for many years in Hamilton. In this case we are once again indebted to Mr. Gardiner for a definite authentication. This type of cane (as explained previously) was described several years before it was acquired, and an instant identification was possible. This specimen is 45″ in length. To reiterate, it is blown from a clear glass into which had been incorporated narrow strips of red, white and blue. The knob is slightly bulbous, and twisted several times where it joins the length of the cane. It has an inner coating of mercury.

A clear *glass pitcher* obtained from Mr. Gardiner. This specimen would normally be listed as a commercial product. Since it was never offered for sale it is included among the special items. Its history provides definite knowledge of techniques and designs used in the Burlington works of Hamilton. It is 9½″ at its highest, and 17¼″ in circumference at the bottom. The slightly tapering body is engraved with a flowing floral design and the letters M. G. It was made for Mary Gardiner (mother of George) by a Mr. Roth, *circa* 1882. According to Mr. Gardiner, this Mr. Roth boarded with the family, and in appreciation of the home-like atmosphere he presented this pitcher to Mrs. Gardiner, Sr. This piece has a metal handle or bail which clips into two applied pressed glass sockets upon which appears the legend "pat May 1880." The mould in which these sockets were cast was apparently so worn that the date is blurred. But the information supplied by Mr. Gardiner more or less establishes it. This piece illustrates several techniques in use at that time in the Burlington works. These are: an applied (separately made) handle consisting of a gather twisted and drawn out so that the bottom half is the heavier; a bottom decorated by means of a mould having a design

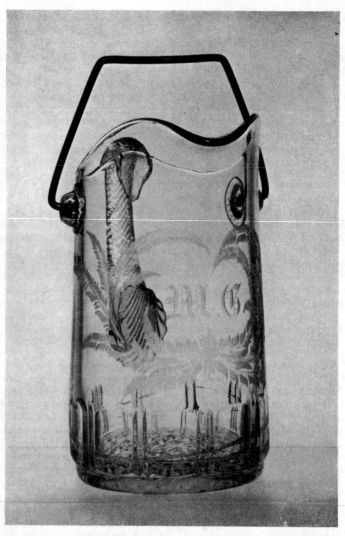

No. 17.  Pressed Flint Glass Pitcher made for Mary Gardiner
at the Burlington Glass Works, 1880-1882.

known as daisy and button (in this case the button is depressed); a moulded panelled base; and the previously mentioned engraving. The technique of twisting used to complete the handle of this piece is typical of that used in the manufacture of such whimseys as drapes and canes.

Three *glass sticks* obtained from Mr. Gardiner are examples of special pieces used by Burlington paperweight makers. The largest and most complete measures 5½" in circumference and the end, still intact, shows that it was made by the use of a pontil rod a full 1½" in diameter. This piece (original length unknown) was made from a very dark amber glass. The second piece is the fragment of a stick consisting of an apparently specially made batch of a very deep aquamarine colour. The third piece is the rounded tip of a stick coloured a rich ruby red. The length is not known, but the circumference would have been about 4¾". The data contained in these chunks is of great importance.

## Lamps and Lighting Equipment

It has been established that many Canadian glass houses manu-factured lamps of various types, the most interesting of which is that known as *L'Ange Gardien* (The Guardian Angel). These little *hand-lamps* are typical of a product made for nineteenth century Quebec. For some years it was thought that these lamps were either imported or made in Montreal glass houses, but study of shards from the Burlington glass house proves that Angel lamps were produced in that establishment. Of course, lamps of a similar type could have been manufactured in several glass houses in Canada or England or both. Indeed, lamps almost identical in size and form may still be purchased from several Montreal firms, and many of the original specimens have been supplied with modern globes, burners and wicks. The latter are difficult to identify but the lamps are not. The reason is that the original lamps were embossed with the following legend "L'Ange Gardien—Extra—C. H. Binks & Co. Montreal," and that C. H. Binks & Co. is a long defunct firm, at least in a sense relative to these little lamps.

Mr. B. Stuart-Stubbs,* then reference librarian of the Redpath Library at McGill University, stated in 1955 that the firm of Charles H. Binks & Co. came into being in 1877-1878. Prior to that date this

*Now associated with the University of British Columbia.

company was listed as Jackson, Binks & Co.   From 1876 to 1899-1900,
C. H. Binks & Co. were listed as importers.   From 1899-1900 to 1904-
1905, Mr. Binks listed his firm as "importers of groceries and druggists
sundries."   The latter listing suggests that this firm dropped all interest
in the Angel lamps at or about the time the Burlington glass house was
in decline.   In any case, the technique employed in making these lamps
is that of the nineteenth rather than the twentieth century.

These little lamps are closely associated with religious ceremonials
in the Province of Quebec.   The coloured glass globes, usually of reds or
green, are not of a type usually encountered elsewhere in the Dominion.
These lamps are 2⅛" in height, and 10" in circumference at the bottom.
They were made in a two-piece mould, and the applied handle is opposite
the name and at right angles to the mould marks.   The colours of glass
used were light and dark amber (typical bottle glass), light and dark
blues, and a clear non-lead glass known in Canada as flint.   Glass in all
these colours, particularly the light blues, is known to have been made at
The Burlington Glass Works.

The globes present many problems in authentication.   Several lamps
have been found with globes made from glass of a deep ruby red.   As these
are plain in design, and a deep ruby is somewhat doubtful as a product of
the Burlington works, these could be classed as modern replacements.
But the blue, green and light red globes—especially those having a slightly
twirled, ribbed design—are quite possibly original.   These globes average
3" in height, and 10⅛" in circumference (see Plate 18).

These little lamps present another problem to collectors in that
several specimens *not* embossed with C. H. Binks' name have been found
with brass fittings made by several firms of manufacturers listed as having
headquarters in the United States.   In several instances such companies'
names have included the term "patented by," and the supposition has
always been that such pieces as are supplied with metal parts manufactured
in the United States were products of that country.   This is not necessarily
the case.   The prototype of a particular item may have been first manufactured in a country in which the patent was first registered; but the
manufacturers of similar products located in foreign countries may—

No. 18.   Lamps (clear base with ruby or deep blue shades).   Burlington Glass
Works.   Vigil Lights (green and deep blue).   Canada Glass House, Montreal.

indeed often did—obtain permission to produce similar pieces.   The best
known instance from a collector's point of view is that of the Colt's
percussion revolvers made in England and supplied to Canadian militia-
men.   The Hamilton Public Library reports that the Burn & Robinson
Manufacturing Company, W. S. Burn, manager, of Hamilton, Ontario,
made parts for lanterns and lamps in 1886.   This firm carried on until
1892, when the name changed to Burn Lantern Company.   In 1893
the firm again changed its name, this time to the Ontario Lantern
Company, and in 1905 it became the Ontario Lantern & Lamp Company.

No. 19.  Lamp with opalescent blue opal glass (milk glass) base, flint
glass bowl and chimney.  Burlington Glass Works, (*Circa 1880*).  Flint
  Glass Lamp and Chimney.  Burlington Glass Works.  (*Circa 1885*).

The inclusion of these data is necessary because of the prevailing idea that Canadian manufacturers did not at any time produce lamps and lamp fittings. It is also a fact that many lamps of a later date made at the Burlington glass house are found with burners stamped—O L & L Co., Banner, etc. Banner was one of the early trade names applied to wick-holding burners manufactured by this company. This firm may be considered to come on the Canadian scene rather late.

A *table lamp* supplied with a burner of a type made in Hamilton and a chimney of a type proven to have been manufactured in the Burlington Glass Works, is an important item of Canadiana. It is authenticated by information received orally and by shards excavated on the site of the Burlington glass house. If it does not have the semi-religious interest of the Binks lamps, it does reveal a much greater command of the medium. From the base to the metal rim it measures 10⅞″. From the base to the top of the chimney it is 21¾″ in height overall. The base (exclusive of the bowl) was made from a fiery opalescent glass known as blue milk-glass. It measures 6¾″ and was made in a four-piece mould by the technique known as "pressed". The bowl was mould blown in a three-piece mould from a clear flint non-lead glass. Both pieces are decorated (see Plate 19) with a design not familiar to this writer, but which indicates a late nineteenth century date. The chimney is interesting and easily authenticated as having been made at the Burlington works. It appears to have been sandblasted by a master, and afterward cut in a floral and leaf design. The peculiar crimp used to finish off the upper rim of this chimney is of a type made by a Burlington blacksmith. This one piece illustrates the techniques of pressing glass, moulding glass, sandblasting and cutting. (See under "shards" for verification of types and colours of glass.)

Another *table lamp* of clear (flint) glass, has a height of 9⅞″. The base was pressed in a two-piece mould, and the bowl was blown in a mould having three sections. Although both base and bowl were worked in moulds having a decoration known as fish scale, there is one important difference: the scale decoration on the base is on the inner side, while that on the bowl is on the outer. The reason for this lies in the techniques used in making the two pieces. A pressed design allows any type of decoration possible by this method to be used on either or both faces of a piece but a blown piece always results in a design on the outer side with a corresponding depression on the inner. In addition to a fish scale, this piece was embellished with a straight ribbed pattern extending around an upright section of the base measuring ⅛″. The chimney acquired with this specimen appears to have been treated to three of the methods of decoration in use at The Burlington Glass Works: cutting, engraving and sandblasting. The cutting wheel was used to supply a continuous leaf design around the centre. The engraving consists of a series of loops, and the sandblasting was quite expertly used to produce four seemingly engraved rings, two above and two below the central decorations. This widely flared chimney is finished off with a typical Burlington crimp.

Many smaller types of *hand-lamps* were made in the Burlington glass house. The general features of these are commonplace with one exception, that of trailed handles.

As may be noted in Plates 19 and 21, The Burlington Glass Works specialized in several types of chimneys, and the various types of crimping or beading used to complete these chimneys suggest that there could be some revision of the dating of chimneys. As has been stated, the Burlington works employed men trained both abroad and in the United States. If so, why do chimneys known to have been made in this glass house *circa* 1895 have such a primitive type of finial? Could the beaded finial on a chimney indicate a very late date? This is an interesting question which remains to be answered.

Since many of the Burlington pieces were produced during the closing decades of the nineteenth century and are now commanding "antique" prices from collectors, it should be of interest to note contemporary asking prices. The Fall and Winter Catalogue No. 28, 1894-1895, of the T. Eaton Co. Ltd. of Toronto was studied for data on lamps and glass in general. In that publication banquet lamps are priced at $2.00, $2.50, $2.75, $3.50 and $5.00, library or hanging lamps with glass fonts and opal domes measuring 14″ at $2.00 (with "decorated dome shade" at $2.50, $3.00, and $4.00). It is upsetting to learn that the hanging lamps decorated with prisms, which many innocent persons buy to hang in "Early Canadian Rooms," were made in 1894 and sold "complete with prisms, latest designs" for $4.50 to $7.75 each, and that prisms for lamps cost only 36c. a dozen. Under the listing "Glass Lamps" are to be found: hand lamps, complete (burner and chimney) at 15c. to 30c. each; stand lamps, complete, at 35c., 50c. and 65c. each; bracket lamps, complete with bracket, were priced at 35c., 50c. and 65c. each.

Under the listing "Glassware" may be found: tumblers, *moulded,*

4c. to 8c. each; tumblers, *pressed*, a special line, 5c. each; tumblers, *lead flint*, engraved, all the latest patterns, $1.00 a dozen; goblets, moulded, 4c. to 8c. each; salt and pepper shakers, decorated, tinted opal glass, 10c. to 15c. each; salt and pepper shakers, nickle screw caps, 5c., 6c. and 7c. each; sugar shakers, ruby and green with silver plated screw tops, special, 25c. each.

The above prices prevailed when Canadian glass houses were producing over a quarter-million dollars worth of glass in one year.

## Geometric and Other Mould-Blown Designs

The terms "mould-blown" and "blown-moulded" are identical in meaning. Both terms indicate that a piece was first shaped by taking a gather of glass and expanding it in a particular mould. This piece was then removed from the mould and manipulated in various ways by use of a pontil rod or punty. The removal of the punty caused the well-known circular scar which, if it were not ground out on a wheel, supplies the evidence of this technique. The only difference between mould-blown and free-blown was the use of a mould.

Later North American techniques included moulded (i.e. blown in a mould but finished by use of a snap), and pressed. The latter designates a piece finished by mechanical means.

The only complete example of what the McKearins term "geometric" design known to have been used in the Burlington glass house is that shown in Plate 20. This interesting item is 3⅜" in height and 6" at the widest in circumference. The design is obtained with a mould having a ribbed decoration used both horizontally and vertically. This piece is finished off with a flared rim obtained by expanding then folding over the excess glass.

Other mould-blown designs used by this glass house include a key pattern, and a very finely ribbed design, both of which are authenticated by means of shards.

## Commercial Novelties:

The first of these is not strictly a novelty. But as it has many times been sold as such it is placed in this category. This little *decanter* measures 3⅛" in height, and has the bulbous body and elongated neck of a true decanter. These were originally made *circa* 1895 for the Imperial Extract

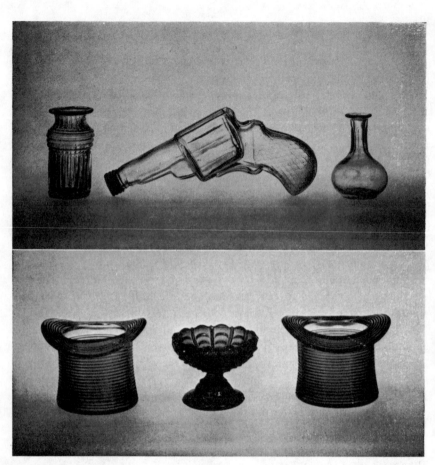

No. 20.  Mould-blown Container (Geometric type). (*Circa 1875*).  Revolver Bottle:
Pressed. (*Circa 1885-1909*).  Pressed Condiment Bottle (Decanter)
made for Imperial Extract Co. (*Circa 1895*)

Pressed Hat (Commercial).  Light amber.
Pressed Miniature Compote (Master Salt).  Deep blue.
Pressed Hat (Toothpick Holder).  Deep amber.
All six specimens made in the Burlington Glass Works.

Co. of Toronto, Ontario, Thos. G. Bright-Francis A. Shirriff (Flavouring Extracts, Essential Oils, etc.). The starred base and the six-sided neck were obtained with a two-piece mould, the flared rim by use of a snap.

*Revolver bottles* were manufactured in great numbers by the Burlington works *circa* 1885-1909. They had many uses, and numbers have been preserved for various reasons. According to information received orally the glass blowers themselves made these bottles to brandish during Labour Day parades. When used commercially, these revolvers were filled with coloured candies and sold to children of all ages. In the commercial product the end representing the muzzle is supplied with a thread on which is screwed a tin cover. These pieces are 8½″ in length and have a typical revolver shape, complete with cylinder, ejector, frame and handle.

The pieces already noticed were made from a clear flint glass. But, as far as has been ascertained, the commercial novelty glass hat made in the Burlington works was made from every type and colour of glass manufactured by that firm. Information received orally has been verified by shards obtained on the site. Such shards provide authentication of small *glass hats* embellished with a horizontally ribbed design. The several colours of glass known to have been made in this glass house provide additional authentication.

The first of these hats is 1⅞″ in height, and resembles in design the piece shown in plate No. 161 of Ruth Webb Lee's *Victorian Glass Handbook*, and termed "Celery vase size." The colour is a pale blue with a very faint greenish tint (a colour found in many nineteenth century ink bottles made in Canada).

The second is similar in all respects, with the one exception that it was made in a two-piece mould from glass of a type and colour used for medicine bottles—a dark amber.

The third authenticated hat is of a somewhat different type. This piece resembles the usual beaver hat of the late 90's in shape, but it lacks the ribbed design. It is a plain hat, 2″ in height, and made from a glass of a peculiar dark blue with a faint tinge of purple.

A *miniature glass compote* (*master salt*), 1¾″ in height, was made in a three-piece mould having a fish scale design. The colour of glass used is similar to that of the preceding piece, and the dark rich blue is typical of the Burlington Glass Works (see Plate 20).

*Pressed Glass Specimens Attributed to the Burlington Works*

Although these pieces are listed as "attributed to," there are several reasons why the attribution is warranted. The source of both specimens was Hamilton, and the data provided orally is in some degree seconded

No. 21.   Pressed Glass Patterns made in the Burlington Glass Works.   Covered butter dishes were an important item in this glass house.

Lamp and Two Chimneys made in the Burlington Glass Works, 1875-1885.   The shards, excavated on the site, allow authentication.

by shards obtained on the site of the Burlington glass house. The term "attributed to" has suffered from misuse, particularly in the arts; but it is necessary because of the great numbers of collector's items which, at the time of manufacture or creation, were not thought to have any future importance and were therefore not signed or marked. The archaeologist and researcher is continually faced with the necessity of taking a stand, and many of the world's leading authorities work from either a literal or mental "sense of touch." The reasons for including the following pieces are given in the text.

A *covered butter dish* of flint glass with an overall height of 5″ and a diameter of 7⅛″. Although the complications of the design are such that the mould marks are almost obliterated, it appears to have been made by pressing in a two-piece mould. The bottom and edge of the base are decorated with an interlocking ring design, and the flared side is furnished with a key pattern. The rounded cover has a band of plain glass, then the key design is repeated. The upper section has the interlocking ring, and the knob is rounded with a bull's eye finial. There are many points to support this attribution, among which are shards verifying the use of this type of glass and the key and bull's eye designs favoured by the Burlington glass makers.

A clear glass two-piece *covered butter dish*, pressed in a mould having four sections. It too was obtained in Hamilton, and was said to have been made in the Burlington works. It has an overall height of 6″, and a diameter of 7¼″. The bottom of the base is decorated with radiating tapered prisms, the wall with a sunken bull's-eye, and the flared rim with a partially ribbed design. The cover wall is half plain and half decorated with 1¼″ bull's-eyes. The flat top is ribbed, and the knob was given four miniature bull's-eyes and a four-pointed finial. The metal in this piece is particularly brilliant.

One important factor in relation to these two pieces is a remark made and repeated by Mr. Gardiner, that "the old works made many covered dishes including those used for butter."

## Specimens Made of Opal Glass Authenticated Orally and by Shards

The author is not a chemist and therefore must depend on more informed authorities. According to the works consulted the 1840-1850 formula for opal glass called for a "small quantity of oxide of tin or, what is better, phosphate of lime, or well-burned bone ash." Mr. Gardiner said that he thought they used "oxides and lime." No doubt modern makers of milk glass have their own formulas. But whatever the chemical composition, the opal glass made in The Burlington Glass Works included many colours and forms. From shards excavated on the site it appears that opal glass salt and pepper shakers were an important commercial product, as were similar dishes, novelties and lamps. One intriguing shard has a bottom section bearing the scar of a pontil rod. What a find a specimen made by this technique would be! The following are the known opal glass specimens, exclusive of the lamp previously noted, made in The Burlington Glass Works.

A hexagonal two-handled *covered sugar dish* 5¼″ in height overall. Both base and cover were pressed in a two-piece mould, the marks of which are quite apparent on the cast handle. As it appears that all pressed glass items must be given a name to designate the design this could be known as the "Fleur-de-Lis and Shell." The fleur-de-lis is self-explanatory; the shell is somewhat similar to that used by Mr. Chippendale. In addition to these is a scroll-like pattern on both base and cover. The knob is round with four lines of beaded decoration. The scrolled handles have a small daisy on each shoulder. When held to the light all edges reveal that the batch of glass from which this specimen was made was what is known as "opalescent" opal glass (i.e., having an iridescent sheen). This piece is shown in Plate 22, and its importance is that it allows the authentication of additional specimens acquired in Canada. Of course, a similar mould may have been used in many Canadian glass houses as well as in others in England and the United States. Conclusions as to the authenticity of glass must be approached with great care.

A *covered creamer* acquired at a later date. This is a companion piece to the sugar bowl and is similar in all respects except those incidental to its being a cream jug with a lip, and the addition of four small daisies. Both pieces were at one time embellished with gilding on upper edges and knobs apparently applied by the manufacturer.

*Opal glass salts and peppers.* The date on which the first salt and/or pepper shaker was introduced is unknown. The larger sugar shaker, especially in silver, preceded the salt shaker by many decades, and it appears that the first salt container used at table was similar to a miniature footed compote or small dish. This being so, we must date the following pieces *circa* 1880-1905. The tops, now somewhat battered, are quite possibly not the originals, since the threading does not seem to match. All are of a type known as "screw top."

No. 22.  Opal (Milk) Glass Salts and Souvenir Pipe made in
the Burlington Glass Works, 1875-1905.

Opal (Milk) Glass items made in the Burlington Glass Works (covered pieces
authenticated by shards excavated on the site).

An *opal salt*, a bulbous specimen with a height of 3″ and a bottom circumference of 8″. The metal used is extremely iridescent, and was pressed in a three-piece mould. The bottom edge of the base was decorated for a width of 1″ with a swirled ribbing and a vine-like leaf design consisting of nine leaves was placed vertically and almost parallel to each mould mark. The screw cap was made of tin.

Another *opal salt*, an urn-like piece made from a true milk-white glass. It was pressed in a most peculiar mould, as the fins or mould marks indicate the use of a two-piece mould for the square base and an irregular five-piece mould for the body. It is 3⅛″ in height, and the upper shoulder, which is beaded, measures 6⅝″ in circumference. It has a tin screw cap.

Another *opal salt*, a hexagonal piece made from a batch having a slight iridescence. It was pressed in a three-piece mould and decorated by a design resembling double beading terminating in a button. It is 2⅞″ in height and 2″ in diameter. It is now equipped with the remains of a screw cap made of tin.

A four-panneled *opal salt* pressed in a mould decorated with a design which may be called a Princess' Feather variant. It is 3″ in height, and the sides at the base measure 1⅝″. The metal is slightly iridescent when examined in cross-section. The cover, obviously a replacement, is a screw cap made from tin.

A *blown Easter egg*. The Burlington glass house manufactured this type of novelty in great numbers. The glass eggs were sold at Easter time, and throughout the year as souvenirs of popular summer resorts. they were usually embellished with a painted or enamelled floral design and an appropriate legend or, when used as souvenirs, with the name of the resort stamped in coloured inks. This authenticated specimen measures 3¾″ in length and 9″ in circumference. These are to be found in some numbers and a variety of sizes throughout the Hamilton area.

An *opal pipe*. It has been well established that pipes were a favourite offhand whimsey of Canadian glass blowers. But, apart from a later type made from rods of prepared glass, which includes cigar and cigarette holders, the only specimens known to remain are commercial pressed pieces produced by several Canadian glass houses. The one specimen obtained in Hamilton was pressed in a three-piece mould. The batch of glass was a milk-white without any iridescence whatsoever. It is 5⅞″ in length and the bowl is 7⅜″ in circumference. The front part of the bowl was decorated with enameled forget-me-nots, and the edge of the bowl and the central section of the stem were painted with gilt bands. Although this is a somewhat commonplace item, it and others like it when authenticated add data to a growing realization of the importance of Canadian glass.

### FACTS LEADING TO AUTHENTICATION

The following summary reviews the factors that make possible the authentication of pieces produced by The Burlington Glass Works:

### PRESSED GLASS PATTERNS USED BY THE BURLINGTON WORKS

Key with Wedding Ring (interlocking circles)
Bull's Eye and variants
Fishscale
Grape and Vine
Daisy and Button (button depressed)
Edges beaded and scalloped

### METHODS OF DECORATION OTHER THAN GLASS

Cutting                Enamelling
Engraving              Painting
Sandblasting           Gilding
Staining

### CLEAR GLASS DESIGNS AUTHENTICATED BY SHARDS*

Key—both pressed and mould-blown
Ribbed and/or Prism—a favourite pattern used horizontally and vertically in mould-blown, moulded and pressed pieces
Stippling—used as a background
Rayed pattern for bases—rayed ribs or prisms, pointed, rounded, or with beads or dots added to either form.
Flute—used on many pieces
Grape and Vine—a design used on tableware
Cane variant—as Plate 132, No. 2, Ruth Webb Lee, "American Pressed Glass"
Daisy variants—frosted and plain
Block with Fan
Oblique basket weave
S pattern

*The terminology is based on that found in Mrs. Lee's *Handbook of Early American Pressed Glass Patterns*.

No. 23.   Flint Glass Berry Set in a grape design.
Burlington Glass Works.   (*Circa* 1898).

Shards, etc., excavated on the site of the Burlington Glass Works.

## DESIGNS IN OPAL (MILK GLASS) AUTHENTICATED BY SHARDS

Princess' Feather variant
Shell
Fleur-de-lis

Crown (finial)
Fan (several sizes)
Scroll

## COLOURS OF GLASS AUTHENTICATED BY SHARDS

Flint (clear—several types)
Green—pale to deep olive (bottle glass)
Amber—pale to deep
Blue—sapphire to ultramarine
Opal—pale custard; white; opalescent white (irides-
    cent amber); "fiery" white (very iridescent
    amber); pale blue; deep blue; opalescent blue

## TECHNIQUES AUTHENTICATED BY SHARDS

Free-blown
Mould-blown (punty used)
Moulded (blown in a mould, finished by use of a
    snap)
Pressed (mechanical)

## CONTAINERS, ETC., AUTHENTICATED BY SHARDS

Ink bottles—two-mould, pressed
Bottles—3 to 4 oz. containing(?) "For the Teeth and Breath,"
    moulded in two-piece moulds
Bottles—1 oz. free-blown (chemists'?)
Flint glass lantern chimneys—large size, moulded in two-piece
    moulds
Moulded and pressed lamps
Covered dishes and dishes
Preserve jars (sealers) and pickle bottles
Bottles of many sizes and weights of metal
Glass alleys (marbles)
Egg cups—pressed with S design on rim
Hats—free blown and pressed
Salt and pepper shakers—opal glass, white to blue, pressed
Covered dishes—opal, flint, pressed
Chimneys—many sizes, blown
Glass tubing—early types

4. The Napanee Glass House, Napanee (1881-1883)

JOHN HERRING (1818-1898) was one of those splendid Canadians whose contribution to Canada cannot be measured in dollars and cents. Although not a native son (he was born in the United States), Herring was typical of those who came to Canada and, with a sincere appreciation of the opportunities offered by an unproven country, gave his talents, his youthful energy, his innate feeling for commerce and, in the end, the greater part of his fortune in an attempt to perform what proved to be an impossible task; the manufacture of window glass with which to brighten and protect the homes of fellow Canadians. Window glass seems to have been manufactured in Canada at an earlier date (see chapter 8), but the first attempt to make it in Ontario was that of John Herring in his glass works in Napanee in 1882.

The information obtained orally by the author in the town of Napanee and from other sources may be supplemented by consulting the following: "John Herring" in *A Cyclopedia of Canadian Biography*, edited by Geo. Maclean Rose, Rose Publishing Company, Toronto, 1886; an obituary of John Herring printed in *The Napanee Beaver*, 1898; *The History of the County of Lennox and Addington*, by Walter S. Herrington, K.C., The Macmillan Company of Canada, Limited, Toronto, 1913; books and articles by the author, including the catalogue of The Edith Chown Pierce and Gerald Stevens Collection of Early Canadian Glass at the Royal Ontario Museum.

John Herring was born on February 17, 1818, at Denmark, Lewis County, New York. His father, William Herring, had emigrated from Devon to the United States in 1810. In 1814 he married Cynthia Buck, of Massachusetts, and moved to Denmark, N.Y., where he became associated with local brewing interests. In 1828 the Herring family moved to a farm in the vicinity of Gouvernour, N.Y., where William lived until his death in 1867. Apparently rural life did not appeal to the young John Herring, so while teaching school during the winter months, he spent his spare time as an apprentice in the construction trade. In 1841, learning of a shortage of trained artisans in Canada, he moved to

Kingston, Canada West, where he designed and built a house for Captain Gildersleeve. From Kingston Mr. Herring moved to Napanee, where he was to remain for the balance of his long and useful life.

John Herring's record as a resident of Napanee begins with his interest in a local foundry. The record suggests that he manufactured the first stoves ever cast in that district. His stove was called Northern Farmer, and had "high elevated ovens." One of the first big jobs undertaken by the Herring foundry was casting the iron pillars for the Kingston City Hall. In the autumn of 1842 he revisited Gouvernour, and while there married Pamelia Fowler, whom he had met while teaching school in Watertown, N.Y. He brought his bride to Napanee, and the record states that "his children were eleven in number, five of whom only reached maturity." By 1860 Herring had been elected to the town council, where he served for almost a quarter of a century. He served as reeve for many years, but because of his many commitments refused the office of mayor. In the meantime, he had added to his business activities such enterprises as "brickmaking, lumbering, and potash manufacturing." In 1857 he began the manufacture of the Buckeye reapers and mowers, several of which were still in use in 1886. In 1864 he returned to his first interest and built the West Ward Academy. After this venture he sold out his interest in the brickmaking business, and concentrated on the foundry. In 1872 he became one of the principal investors in an establishment to manufacture paper. In 1876 he met one of his first reverses which, in the end, proved to be an asset—the forming of a company to provide street lighting for Napanee with gas obtained from petroleum. And now we come to that period pertinent to this work—The Napanee Glass Works.

According to the best sources, the Napanee glass house was first conceived in 1880. In that year it was proposed that an establishment for the manufacture of window glass be erected in the town of Napanee. The initiators of this project are not known, but John Herring was one of the first to look into the matter. The proposed company was to have a capital of $200,000, but for various reasons those first interested dropped out of the enterprise and Herring decided to go on alone. In the following year, 1881, he visited glass houses in the United States, including those located in Pittsburgh and Syracuse, and arriving home he erected the

Napanee glass works.   According to *A Cyclopedia of Canadian Biography*, the Napanee project to manufacture window glass was "the only establishment of the kind in the Dominion."   This could be questioned, as it is known that several glass houses in and about Montreal had made or contemplated the making of broad or window glass.   At any rate, the Napanee venture was the first of its kind in Ontario.

Mr. Herring was a classic example of the energetic man who extends his interests beyond his knowledge.   The mystery and glamour surrounding the making of glass apparently attracted this hard-headed business man.   But John Herring knew nothing about glass-making, and from the first experienced a great deal of trouble with his employees. It is possible that his glass blowers were affiliated with that all-important group the Glass Bottle Blowers Association of the United States and Canada, for the record states that the operatives were controlled by the glass-makers' union.   A later record states that he imported German glass blowers and workmen from the United States.   It is possible that the German glass blowers would not agree to join the union, and that friction arose among the employees.

At any rate, we know that the attempt to manufacture window glass in Napanee was a failure, and that Herring attempted to recoup his losses by producing such articles as were not mass-produced but made to orders obtained by travelling salesmen.   Personal interviews with members of the Herring family revealed that globes for street lights were produced in the Napanee glass house in 1883, and other sources told of the manufacture there of druggist's wares.   Such items were of course only a rather desperate attempt at survival.   In 1883, Herring was obliged to close the glass works, after manufacturing for two seasons. He turned out a quality of glass such as had never been in use in Canada, and which aimed to control the Dominion market to the exclusion of imported articles.   Herring made an attempt in 1884 to form a joint stock company for the purpose of reopening the works, but owing partly to the tightness of the money market, though principally to his lack of practical knowledge of the business, he was unable to succeed.   In 1885 the people of the town combined with Mr. Herring and sent a man to England to try and raise capital, with the hope of expanding the works to at least three times its former capacity. But this attempt also was a failure, and the glass house at Napanee never rekindled its fires. The last batch had been made, and this gallant attempt came to an end, leaving a limited number of desirable items for future collectors of Canadian glass.

Mr. Herring, although he had suffered financial loss, continued to be an outstanding citizen, supplying jobs through his other enterprises to those seeking employment. Contemporary records state, "He is still one of the largest employers of labour and heaviest ratepayers in town; and we do not know of a man whose loss would be more deeply felt than his."

The location of the Napanee glass house was "nearly opposite the Grand Trunk Depot," according to the *History of the County of Lennox and Addington* (page 235). This is confirmed in the obituary of Mr. Herring, which places it "just north of the Grand Trunk station in this town."

The late Edith Chown Pierce, to whom the author is indebted for much of the data relative to Napanee, wrote in her *Canadian Glass: A Footnote to History*, (privately printed, The Ryerson Press, Toronto, 1954):

The factory was started by John Herring, and was located north of the railway station, then the Grand Trunk. Mrs. Mabel L. Ward, Mr. Herring's granddaughter, of Oakville (Ontario), to whom I wrote, was eighty-three years old in June, 1953. . . . The Herring glass works produced a fine quality of glass, and employed a large number of men. It is recorded that he (Herring) brought expert glass-makers from Germany, Belgium, France and England at various times to instruct his local workmen. The men lived in specially built houses in a sort of community of their own, on the Selby Road near the glass works. They made window glass, and the workmen, as in Mallorytown, indulged in whimseys—canes, candlesticks, glass hats, bowls and pitchers. Writing about her grandfather, Mrs. Ward says: "My grandfather had Yankee ingenuity, but was very stubborn, and went into the manufacture of glass against the advice of his friends. The locale was not to his advantage, and he had to import everything he used*, as well as the foreign glass blowers."

Mrs. Pierce spent several years in an attempt to gather authentic data relative to the Napanee glass works, and her brochure (now a collector's

*See also *Historic Kingston, No. 3, November, 1954, article 5*, "Early Canadian Glass."

item) contains additional information on pieces and types produced by that house. The following is an excerpt from page 10:

Among the whimseys made at Napanee, besides glass canes, were flowers and whorls of various kinds. . . . I have been able to acquire three Napanee candle sticks in cottage lustre (mercury glass), all of the same design, but two perfectly matched, a glass cane, and a large piece of raw glass (just as it came from the pots), that had been used. . . as a door stop.

The author, in collaboration with Mrs. Pierce, made several visits to Napanee in search of data. These trips were not too rewarding, but they did establish that window glass had been attempted, that it had been a failure because of the materials used, and that the glass house had turned to other items. The "cottage lustre" candlesticks in particular are specimens which have been authenticated as products of Napanee. It is true that a prototype—some with coloured sockets—was produced in Austria, but the imported specimens are so marked. The "chunks" mentioned by Mrs. Pierce are to be found in a number of homes in and about Napanee. These are large pieces of raw glass, usually aquamarine in colour, typical of glass houses producing glass from local materials.

In the case of Napanee, chance revealed the source of the silica-bearing Potsdam sandstone used by this house. The author, in an attempt to obtain data about the Mallorytown glass house, advertised in local papers and got in touch with numbers of local residents. Among the latter were Mr. William Armstrong and Miss Sarah-Ann Armstrong of Lansdowne, Ontario, with whom he had an instructive interview. They told him that their grandfather, William Armstrong (deceased 1882) had sold a sandstone quarry to "a gentleman from Napanee," and that elderly residents of the Lansdowne area had spoken of great caravans of horses and wagons coming to the quarry, taking on loads of stone blocks, and returning to the railroad at Lansdowne, where flat-cars were loaded with this stone to be sent to Napanee. Although somewhat confused as to dates, the Armstrongs, brother and sister, were correct in their data, and provided the location of the quarry: Lot 21, 2nd concession, Township of Lansdowne, County of Leeds, Ontario.*

*See analysis of Potsdam sandstone in Chapter 1.

No. 24.   Two druggist's jars with covers from The Napanee Glass House.   Goblet
from The St. John's Glass House, St. John's, P.Q.
Lamp chimney, Burlington Glass Works.

Another authentic and worthwhile find resulted from an interview
with the late Daniel L. Walsh, of Brockville, Ontario.   Mr. Walsh was a
druggist of the old school who had served his apprenticeship in several
of the oldest extant drug stores in the country of Leeds, as well as other
districts.   In one of these establishments, which dated from the early
1800's, Mr. Walsh had worked for a man who had told him of a traveller
dropping in with a small bar of glass in a wooden holder, explaining that

the bar was a sample of the glass made at Napanee, and asking for orders for druggist's jars, retorts, etc.   According to Mr. Walsh, the proprietor had ordered several dozen jars and some clinical pieces.   The location of this store was obtained from Mr. Walsh, and a visit was made to the present owner.   It was a more than pleasant surprise to find some numbers of blown druggist's jars of a kind typical of Canadian glass houses: jars of a non-lead glass bearing the scar of a pontil rod (such jars as were imported from England were made from a lead glass and the pontil mark was invariably ground off and polished.)   The author acquired a number of these glass jars, several of which were added to the Edith Chown Pierce and Gerald Stevens Collection.

As is usual with nineteenth century glass houses in Canada, the Napanee works have through the years generated a certain amount of what might be classed as folklore.   This class of information has in the opinion of the writer resulted in a small number of unimportant items being attributed to this house.   It has been said that the imported German glass blowers attempted to manufacture glass ornaments in their homes. But the stories of this type appear to have been obtained from persons who do not understand the problems confronting a private individual attempting the manufacture of glass in the 1880's.

As has been stated, Mrs. Pierce was particularly interested in the Napanee works, and much of the information relative to its wares was obtained through her efforts.   She traced its history, frequently visited the area, and was successful in authenticating the mercury glass candlesticks.   Although it was not necessary, a splendid cross-check of the candlesticks was provided when a dust-covered specimen, containing the stub of a candle, was discovered among the druggist's jars known to have been made at Napanee.


AUTHENTICATED SPECIMENS

Five mercury glass candlesticks have been identified.

The author is not familiar with the technique used 'to produce that type of decoration known as mercury glass.   In an attempt to discover the means by which this effect was obtained we approached that expert,

Mr. George Gardiner of Hamilton, who had himself used this technique in the manufacture of glass canes. According to Mr. Gardiner, a glass blower worked and shaped a piece until it was completed; then, freeing the pontil rod and using some means to hold the item, the glass worker poured a small amount of mercury (quicksilver) into the opening left by the removal of the pontil rod. The mercury was "shaken around," and the excess was poured out of the opening. It appears that all this was done while the piece was still warm and before it was annealed. The author does not vouch for this technique but merely adds it to the record. All known authenticated specimens of mercury glass candlesticks manufactured at Napanee appear to be treated in this manner.

The largest of these is 10½″ in height and 4⅜″ across the base. The techniques used in its manufacture are similar to those used in all known specimens. The base and stem are free blown, and both were given an inner coating of mercury. The socket into which the candle fits is of clear glass, decorated on the underside with a Key design, and the rim is serrated. The glass from which this piece was made has a slight aquamarine tint. The bases of these pieces are stepped, and the stems may be classed as baluster or balustroid (i.e., having turnings used in wood working or cabinetmaking).

The second and third candlesticks in the collection are of similar technique. The height of each is 7¾″, but the basic glass is clear.

The fourth and fifth candlesticks are 9″ in height and, excepting the difference of the moulded design on the underside of the rim of the socket, resemble the other three. The design on these suggests a continuous vine, or Tree of Life pattern. Although quite a few of these candlesticks in the Key pattern have been found, the two specimens decorated with the Tree pattern are unique. These were discovered in the Province of Quebec. It is possible that the Tree design has some religious significance and was devised for the Quebec trade. The moulded sockets on all specimens were made in a two-piece mould probably resembling that used for cup plates. These candlesticks are well worth study, as they represent several techniques used in combination to obtain a specific result. The author feels that these pieces were a final attempt of the Napanee glass house to capitalize on techniques and forms introduced by foreign labour.

The largest of the *druggist's jars* obtained through the lead supplied by Mr. Walsh is 8⅞″ in height and 5¾″ in diameter. The jar itself is free blown and is decorated with two applied rings of solid glass. The cover is 3⅞″ in height, and was made in a two-piece mould. The finial is circular and stepped.

No. 25.   Candlesticks (mercury glass: heights, 7¾″, 9″ and 10½″).
Napanee Glass House.

A second jar is 11″ in height, and was free blown without added decoration.  The stopper was made in a two-piece mould.  The finial is flattened.

A third jar, typical of several specimens obtained from the previously mentioned source, is 6⅛″ in height, is free blown, and has a blown moulded stopper similar to the preceding item.

The *solid glass cane* in the Napanee section of the Edith Chown Pierce and Gerald Stevens Collection is an interesting example of a type made in every Canadian glass house during the closing decades of the nineteenth century.  The authentication of this type of whimsey must be approached with great care as the source is difficult to trace.  Indeed, glass canes have always presented a challenge to researchers sincerely interested in authentication since canes of various types have been and are still being imported. Glass canes manufactured in England, France or the United States are not Canadiana. They are merely commercial articles made for export by modern glass houses, and imported by unscrupulous antique dealers interested only in sales. It is better to obtain a specimen from a personal source than from a dealer known to be an importer. This is merely a cautionary hint to those who may attempt further research on Canadian glass. The author has studied glass hatchets (known to have been produced in Canada), glass canes (made in many Canadian glass houses), glass hats (made as both whimseys and commercial items by several Canadian glass houses), and glass swords (said to have been made in The Burlington Glass Works), without adding such items to the Collection because of discoveries made as to their sources. In other words, novelties made from glass are still being manufactured abroad. The source from which a specimen was obtained, the locality in which it was discovered, the quality and type of glass and the manner in which it was made must all be taken into consideration.

The author has received a great number of letters asking for information relative to glass canes. It appears that hundreds of these canes are owned by Canadian collectors, and that each collector feels that his or her glass cane is a unique item. A general answer would be: glass canes are not usually included in serious collections unless known to have been manufactured in a specific glass house by an authentic glass worker. The original McKearin collection, possibly the finest of its kind in North America, included many glass canes in the section showing "fakes."

## 5. The Toronto Glass Company, Toronto (1894-1900)

THE ESTABLISHMENT of this glass house provided Canadian collectors with seemingly endless interesting data. These led to the authentication of several items, and have provided a documented list of glass workers.

In the *Colonial Advocate*, December 9, 1830, there is an advertisement of the British Museum, York (Toronto), U.C. This private museum, owned by William Wood, was situated at the corner of Market Lane, on the west side of Market Square. In addition to "Natural and Artificial

Curiosities, a Cosmorama and a Phantasmagoria," the proprietor an-
nounced that "Mr. Smith, the Fancy Glass blower," is engaged for the
season, and that this exhibition of his art is truly wonderful.

An earlier advertisement, November 17, 1830, reads in part:

Mr. Wood, anxious to gratify a very liberal and generous public,
respectfully begs to inform them, owing to the numerous calls for GLASS
WORK, he has re-engaged Mr. Smith, The Fancy Glass Blower, for a
few days longer.  Mr. Smith will, on the shortest notice, accommodate
Ladies and Gentlemen with any of the following, or almost any other
FANCY GLASS CURIOSITIES, viz:-Birds, Deer, Dogs, Ships, Glass
Pens, &c. &c.

It would be interesting to obtain an authentic example of Mr. Smith's
"curiosities."  Many so-called glass blowers, operating in side-shows at
country fairs, have produced birds, beasts and ships.  Blobs having
nothing to do with commercial glass-making in Canada, and these novelties
are obtainable in some numbers.

The next indication of glass-making in Toronto is an entry in the
*Canada Directory*, 1857-1858, which lists "Langley, Edward, glass factory,
Niagara near Tecumseh St."  The Edward Langley Glass Factory is
not listed in Toronto *Directories* for 1856, or for 1859-1860.  Apparently
Mr. Langley did not have an authentic glass works or, if he did, was
unsuccessful.  He may have been a "fancy glass blower" of the type of
Mr. Smith.

In the years following the 1850's, up to and after the turn of the
century, Canada directories, Toronto directories, Provincial directories,
and other types of publications list many different firms under the
heading of glass manufacturers.  Indeed, the *Might 5 Cities Directory* of
1895, and the *Toronto Directory* of 1897, attempt to establish a great
number of glass-makers who, investigation shows, did not make glass
but only dealt in it; Pilkington Brothers is so listed.   There are a number
of Toronto houses that did make glass but came on the scene quite late
and did not, as far as we can discover, produce anything of importance to
collectors. These include the Diamond Glass Company and the Jefferson
Glass Company, both of which were apparently absorbed by the present
Dominion Glass Company.

There were several additional glass houses established by men who had obtained their training in the Burlington glass house of Hamilton. The most important of these, situated at Port Colborne, Ontario, is said to have produced several types of containers. Another, which had little success, was opened in Dundas, Ontario. There were also, in and about the city of Hamilton, several one-man attempts by hopeful types who purchased used glass and attempted the manufacture of glass containers from straight cullet; the resulting glass was uniformly sad and bubbly.

In addition to the glass houses of Toronto, there were the several working glass houses (most of which are mentioned in the text), that combined to form the Dominion Glass Company Limited. The reasons for this amalgamation, and its later affects on Canadian glass-making, comprise a history in themselves, but its commercial products are not as yet interesting to collectors or historians. Special items of the whimsey type produced by glass blowers in the employ of Dominion Glass are always interesting, however, and the commercial product of today may well be the collector's quarry of the future—providing, of course, some record of an authenticating nature is kept.

A letter received in March, 1957, from Robert H. Blackburn, Chief Librarian of the University of Toronto, states:

The first mention of the Toronto Glass Co. (presumably the same as Toronto Glass Works) is in the 1894 *Toronto Directory* where their address was given as "S. S. Blair cor. Abell." This entry is repeated in 1895 and 1896. They are listed under the address "S. S. Armour cor Abell" for 1897 and 1899. The Ontario Archives, who have the volume for 1900, tell us they are listed there but they do not appear in our volume for 1901.

Oral information supports the accuracy of this. Our informant suggests that this Toronto company was established by several of the senior glass blowers working in the Burlington glass house at Hamilton. Apparently friction arose and outside interests gained control, with the end result that the house ceased operations and the workers were absorbed by glass companies located in both Ontario and Quebec. Although short-lived, the Toronto works employed several of Canada's most accomplished glass blowers, including James Canty and George Gardiner, as well as those in the following documented list from the *Toronto Directory* for 1897.

This list is by no means complete, as it includes only those persons who claimed to be associated with the Toronto works. It was quite usual for nineteenth century directories to list many artisans whose names would be of interest to researchers as labourers, either because of lack of precise information or because he or she "boarded out" and did not appear on tax lists.

## LIST OF PERSONS ASSOCIATED WITH THE TORONTO WORKS IN 1897

John Watt, president, (H-89) (T-97)
John C. Malcolmson, gaffer, (H-89) (T-97)
Geo. A. Bard, blower, (H-89) (T-97)
Jeremiah Behan, blower, (H-89) (H-95) (T-97)
Alfred Bennett, blower, (T-97)
W. H. Betzner, shipper, (T-97)
Wm. F. Chapman, clerk, (T-97)
Saml. Dolman, blower, (H-89) (H-95) (T-97)
Silas Dunton, worker, (T-97)
W. B. Griner, blower, (H-89) (T-97)
Willis Ide, carpenter, (T-97)
John Ling, labourer, (T-97)

John McNichol, blower, (H-89) (H-97) (T-97)
Tom McNichol, blower, (H-95) (T-97)
Theodore Mahon, blower, (T-97)
James F. Malcolmson, worker, (T-97)
W. A. Mitchell, worker, (T-97)
Alex R. Murphy, (T-97)
Thomas Murphy, worker, (T-97) (H-99)
Martin Nolan, blower, (H-89) (H-95) (T-97)
John Schwab, grinder, (T-97)
Peter Schwab, fireman, (T-97)
T. W. Snowdon, blacksmith, (T-97)
Albert Sprigley, packer, (T-97)
Patrick Wickham, blower, (H-95) (H-97) (T-97) (M-99)

## AUTHENTICATED SPECIMENS

Many, if not all, of the men listed as blowers or workers were at one time associated with the Diamond Glass Company, which had branches in several Canadian cities, and were sent when necessary from glass house to glass house to instruct apprentices in the various techniques. In this manner items such as paperweights were produced by the same individuals in different localities. Thus we find that the typical "green house" weight, with a name written on an opal field, was made by Patrick Wickham in cities as far apart as Montreal, Toronto and Hamilton, and we know Wickham worked also at Wallaceburg.

The only item made by the Toronto works, at first, was an aqua-marine-coloured bottle glass produced in a single tank furnace. Under a new management this was replaced by clear or flint glass, but bottles and containers of several sizes and types continued to be the main output. The only commercial item of importance to collectors produced in this

No. 26.  Cast (Commercial) Flint Glass Paperweight stained blue.  Toronto Glass Company, (*Circa* 1897).  Free-blown Paperweight made by Patrick (Pat) Wickham.  Aquamarine bottle glass.  Toronto Glass Company  1895.

works was a cast glass paperweight, made for local Toronto firms.  Several such weights have been discovered.  Although unimportant and far from being works of art, they are nineteenth century Canadiana, and as such are worth recording.

One last note on cast glass paperweights.  There are many available.  Some, which have pasted-in pictures showing Canadian scenes or persons, have little cultural value or any importance for the collector, and were made in both Canada and the United States for the souvenir trade.  One class of cast paperweight which is of interest, however, is the weight made in an early twentieth century Canadian glass house for a specific reason— person or place—and marked by a technique other than a pasted-in picture.  Possibly the most interesting example of this type is one said to have been made in the Toronto Glass Company for the Hobbs Glass Company.  Although it did not make glass itself, Hobbs is sometimes found listed under manufacturers. It is now affiliated with the Pittsburgh Plate Glass Company of Pittsburgh, U.S.A., and in Toronto at least is no longer known by the original name.

A *cast glass paperweight* manufactured in the Toronto Glass Co.'s works for "Nasmith's Business Mens Lunch Counters, with branches at 68 Jarvis, 51 King St. E., 51 King St. W., and 152 Yonge St., Toronto." The date of this commercial but interesting weight could very well be 1897, as the directory for that year lists "The Nasmith Company (Ltd.), John D. Nasmith President, Steam Bakery and Lunch Counters." The directory also includes the four branches indicated by the weight. Earlier directories, such as that of 1885, merely list "Mr. Nasmith, Baker, 68 Jarvis." The weight itself has the typical paperweight form, and is 1¼" in height with a circumference of 9½". It was cast in a two-piece mould. The legend was inscribed by means of a cut-out stencil and sandblasting, the blanked area being stained blue. The Toronto works produced many weights of this type, and all may be authenticated by reference to directories.

A *blown non-commercial glass paperweight*, described in chapter 3. It is the Della Hollyman weight made for Mrs. George Gardiner in 1898, and was the work of Patrick (Pat) Wickham.

A *blown non-commercial glass paperweight*, a typical example of the weights produced by Pat Wickham, 1¾" in height and 2⅞" in diameter. It is made from a gather obtained during the days when the Toronto works manufactured only an aquamarine-coloured bottle glass. It is inscribed "Lizzie Wilkes" and dated 1895. Toronto directories show that a Miss Lizzie Wilkes lived in Toronto during the last decade of the nineteenth century. As has been noted, this weight illustrates the techniques used by Patrick Wickham, and allows authentication of additional examples that may be found throughout Ontario and Quebec. Mr. Wickham always used a blue-green bottle glass to produce the body or cover for his weights, an opal (milk glass) rectangular strip on which to inscribe the name of the person for which the weight was being made, a lead pencil to write the name (sometimes the person for whom the weight was made wrote her own name), a free blown technique necessitating the use of a pontil rod, and, on occasion, a grinding wheel in an attempt (seldom successful) to remove the scar of the pontil rod.

A *typical Wickham glass paperweight*, 1½" in height and 3" in diameter. It was made for "T. (or L.) Milne" in the year 1897. Here again we have the aquamarine bottle glass, the opal field, the attempt to grind out the scar of the pontil rod, etc.

A *free blown glass paperweight* by Patrick Wickham, somewhat larger in size (it measures 1 7/8″ in height and 11 1/2″ in circumference), was made for Miss Lily Brown, Toronto, Ont. Although a typical example of this glass blower's technique, it appears that Miss Brown herself wrote the legend. Determining the identity of Miss Brown is a fascinating example of the sort of sleuthing that research into Canadiana involves. The *Toronto Directory* for 1897 lists Brown, Miss Lilly, opr American Over-gatter Co, b 40 Argyle, and a Miss Lilly E. (Brown), clk T. Eaton Co., (John St.?).

A *clear (flint) glass drape*. The lead for this particular item was supplied by Mr. George Gardiner. According to Mr. Gardiner, a glass blower by the name of James Canty had been employed by the Diamond Glass Company in both The Burlington Glass Works and the Toronto Glass Company in the closing decades of the nineteenth century. Mr. Gardiner stated that Mr. Canty (the spelling of the name "Canty" was supplied by Mr. Gardiner) was "pretty good," and that he had made "several glass drapes." The writer approached the family of the late Mr. Canty and discovered that Mr. Gardiner had been correct. Such drapes as were made by Mr. Canty—and it appears that there were several—were produced *circa* 1899, when the Toronto works had added flint glass to its bottle glass production. The one remaining example of Mr. Canty's attempts at whimseys is a clear glass drape which has been added to the Edith Chown Pierce and Gerald Stevens Collection.

I was able to obtain a tape recorded interview with Mr. George Arthur Shakley of Toronto who was for many years a glass blower working in the United States and Canada and who in 1912 or 1913 moved to Toronto where he worked for the Jefferson Glass Company. Mr. Shakley said, "The personnel of the Jefferson Glass Co. was comprised of Americans and Canadians, the latter coming from Montreal (Diamond Flint Glass) and the Toronto Glass Works." Once again we find that commingling of workers and techniques which causes confusion to the collector. Mr. Shakley mentioned designs used by Toronto glass houses, and he produced several items of his own handiwork including a blown paperweight of the swirl type, coloured glass watch chains, and commercial table wares of the design named "Chippendale" in Canada and "Crystal" in the United States. His information has all been cross-checked.

The author admits that the list of special pieces made in the Toronto Glass Works is inadequate and incomplete. The vast majority of the jars and containers produced by this house are not recorded, and the list of names associated with this works includes many who are known to have had the ability to make almost anything from glass—paperweights, hats, drapes, canes, swords, and pieces both coloured and clear.

### 6. The Beaver Flint Glass Co., Toronto (1897-1948)

THE BEAVER FLINT GLASS COMPANY was one of the few Canadian glass houses which, under its original name, continued operations well into the twentieth century.   There appear to have been many such houses, but, with the amalgamation resulting in the present-day Dominion Glass Company, many late nineteenth century glass houses were swallowed up and their identity lost in the new company.   With the Beaver works it was otherwise.   Toronto city directories from 1897 to 1946 show the name of this house and tell its story.

The *Toronto Directory* of 1897 records that the Beaver Flint Glass Company was located at 50-52 Winchester, corner Parliament.   The president was Mr. J. F. (G.?) Simpson, the Vice-President Mr. J. D. Wright, the Manager and Secretary Treasurer Robt. W. Lowden. Mr. Lowden continued his connection with this firm up to the year 1935.

The *Toronto Directory* for 1897 lists the above officers and such workers as claimed to be associated with this establishment.   The names of the workers were:

| | |
|---|---|
| Miss Maria Adams, forelady | Alfred S. Jones, blower |
| Jos. E. Batchelor, blower | Wm. Lashley, blower |
| Joseph Berry, foreman | Stuart Lowden, blower |
| Lewis Doughty, blower | Samuel Pettit, blower |
| Hercules W. Griffiths, blower | Wm. A. Stark, blower |
| Elias Griner, blower | Wm. Willis, blower |

It is interesting to note that the names of several of the glass blowers included in the list are similar to those of other persons associated with the glass industry.   This confirms what was already known, that glass-making had a strong attraction for persons of a certain type and that glass-making ran in the family.*   The family names in question are: Stuart

*A statement made by Mrs. Wm. Campbell of St. Johns, P.Q.—see chapter 10.

Lowden (R. W. Lowden, Secretary-Treasurer of Beaver Flint Glass); Elias Criner (W. D. "Bard" Griner of both the Hamilton and Burlington glass houses of Hamilton); Alfred S. Jones (Thomas Jones of the Burlington works of Hamilton and the St. Lawrence Glass Works of Montreal, P.Q.; James Jones of the Hamilton works). This interesting point was brought to our attention by Mr. George Gardiner, who had worked with and known many, if not all, of the glass blowers working in Ontario *circa* 1890-1910, in his capacity as secretary of the Glass Blowers Association.

Additional data relative to the same year (1897) shows that the Beaver works were "Manufacturers and Importers of Druggists', Chemists' and Scientific Glassware," "Specialities—Homeopathic Vials, Glass Tubing, All Styles of Glass Syringes, Screw Cap Vials, Test Tubes and Special Chemical Appliances." The years 1898-1900 added bottles and jars to the items in the original list. In 1905 the Beaver works advertised several new items, which included "Prescription Ware, Panels, etc." The name of Mr. Lowden continued to be associated with the firm.

In 1910 the address was given as "Office and Factory, 547 Pare St." From 1910 to 1915 the address and wares remained the same, but Mr. R. W. Lowden became managing director. By 1925 Mr. Lowden was president and manager, and Miss Ina R. Lowden was secretary. In 1930 Mr. Lowden was president. By 1935 he was still president and managing director, but Roberta S. Lowden had become secretary-treasurer. Through the 1940's the firm was listed under "Physicians & Hospital Supplies, 94 Winchester St." 1948 was its last listing.

One of the items manufactured by this works during the 1898-1900 period was a screw-top preserve jar. It appears that this was made in great numbers and in several sizes, but that which is most often encountered is a pint sealer bearing an embossed beaver—the trade mark of this company.

The sealer (eastern Ontario) or preserve jar (western Ontario) is, next to window glass, the most common type of glass found in rural areas; and, until the introduction of the tin can, one of the most important to the housewife. Although these have never been of interest to collectors, their vast numbers alone warrant a few remarks.

No. 27.   Flint Glass Container ("Sealer") made in the
Beaver Flint Glass Company.   (*Circa* 1898).

The only certain method of dating these jars is to find a specimen bearing the name of a specific glass house which was known to have gone out of business at a certain date. In this manner it would be established that a jar was made prior to the day on which the glass works ceased operations, which date could be that day less one. This caution is necessary because certain crude jars suggesting a very early manufacture are known to have been made much later than well made screw-top specimens. The first preserve jar would of course have had a home-made cover. Next came a jar supplied with a metal wire-like band to which a metal loop was fastened; the metal loop could of course be forced over a plug fashioned from cork, glass, etc. The third stage is more difficult to determine, as it could have been either or both of two methods. The earliest appears to be the metal clamp made to hold a flat glass cover, and associated with jars made in the Hamilton works as early as 1866. The only difficulty is that glass covers dating in the early 1860's, and seemingly made to be held in place by a screw-threaded band similar to those in use today, have been found in some numbers. In other words, colour of glass, method used to fasten the cover and apparent age mean little. The only certain means of dating glass jars is to look for a trade-mark or a name, and to know the dates of the glass works in question.

## 7. THE SYDENHAM (DOMINION) GLASS COMPANY LIMITED, WALLACEBURG (1894 — )

MOST OF THE information relative to this Canadian glass house was supplied by Mr. E. G. Davies, manager of the Wallaceburg Works of the Dominion Glass Company Limited. Mr. Davies, a glass-man for many years, has been associated with the Dominion Glass Company in many capacities, and has had experience in several glass houses, including those of Montreal and Wallaceburg.

Although some attempt has been made to interest Canadian collectors in Canadian glass, the Canadian public has little accurate knowledge of the techniques and methods used by nineteenth century glass blowers, or, for that matter, of those used in the first and second decades of the twentieth.   The author has repeatedly stressed the fact that many of the early (pre-1850) techniques were in use as late as 1915-1920, if not later. This fact is confirmed in a letter received from Mr. Davies dated January 14, 1959:

Under separate cover, I am sending you two blow pipes [shown in Plate 28].   The large one is what was used in the manufacturing of chimneys. No doubt you are aware of the process [used] in making chimneys.   This blow pipe is put into the bootleg (smaller secondary furnace), and rests on what is known in glasshouse language as a "pig" [see "dropping the pig," page 38].   The gatherer (apprentice glass blower) revolves the tube (iron: i.e. blow pipe) manually and accumulates sufficient glass for what is required to make the piece of [glass] ware.   It is subsequently marvered (worked) on a polished cast iron slab in order to develop a parison (a blown gather of metal).   At this point, the pipe and the proper piece of glass is handed to the blower (qualified glass blower) who blows up the chimney and also swings it with respect to length, etc.   The blower opens the heel with a special pair of tools.   The neck is creased and broken off by the blower.   A crimping boy picks up the piece of glass (chimney) in a pair of spring snaps [see chapter 2, page 30], and places the neck into a glory hole (small furnace used during the frequent reheating necessary for the completion of a piece of glass) to reheat it.   Subsequent to this, it is crimped (individual crimps establish a specific source) on what is known as a crimping machine.   This completes the making of a chimney.   Due to the fact that chimneys are reheated in the process, it is seldom necessary to anneal (gradually cool) them.

The smaller pipe is used for the making of ordinary bottles.   The blower accumulates the glass on the end of the pipe from the bootleg, marvers it in a polished steel (cast iron) plate and places it into an open and shut mould (two or more piece mould).   The blower blows it up and the result is a container which takes on the impression of the mould. There remains the finish, or ring, to be put on.   This is done by reheating the neck (by use of a snap) and utilizing a tool which puts on any desirable shape of the ring.   The bottles are taken out of the mould and annealed in the usual way.

No. 28.   The Old Sydenham Glass Factory, showing Flint House.(Photo taken in 1898).

Mr. Davies' letter continues with a statement which might be considered one of the most important contained in this work: "I might state that there are no (glass) blowers being employed in Canada at the present time (1959).   Our last hand-blowing operation at this plant was about 1942." (The author has been told that a branch of Dominion Glass located in Montreal still employs an aged glass blower to test an occasional batch.)

The history of the Wallaceburg glass house begins with a poster published in that town in 1891, calling for a meeting to discuss the establishment of a factory for the making of glass. The poster read: *"Public Meeting.* Public Meeting of the citizens interested in establishing a GLASS WORKS in Wallaceburg will be held in the TOWN HALL on WED. EV'G, MAR. 11th at 8 o'clock, p.m. A FULL ATTENDANCE REQUESTED. 1891."

A pamphlet which was mailed to anyone requesting data on glass-making in Wallaceburg was entitled *Wallaceburg: The Glasstown since 1891.* The fact is that glass was not produced in Wallaceburg until 1894. The three-year difference is explained by the time intervening between the first meeting and the first batch of glass produced.

The pamphlet (printed in Wallaceburg) states:

IN THE BEGINNING . . . an Englishman of vision—Captain J. W. Taylor—is actually credited with providing the initial motive that led to the creation of the industry which brought to Wallaceburg in later years the title of Glass Town. The idea of a glass factory was conceived in Captain Taylor's mind when he saw huge deposits of sand along the shores in the lake area through which he piloted various steam craft.

So strongly was Captain Taylor convinced that the sand of the district would be suitable for manufacture of glass, that he was not long in securing the interest and enthusiastic support of such men as Dr. George Mitchell, Dr. W. Hay, Capt. J. W. Steinhoff, D. A. Gordon, J. Gordon, J. Cooper, A. Gordon, D. A. Shaw, M. J. Hurley and others in putting his idea into creation.

As the result of many conferences the above men became convinced of the public success of such an industry and, following efforts to bring it into being, a splendid site was selected . . . for rail and deep-water navigation services. It was the site of the former Patterson Saw Mills. . . . As some of the preliminary work went forward the village folk became quite enthusiastic and lent every effort in support . . ., particularly since it would give employment to the many who were being affected by the slackening lumber trade.

In search of more technical advice Capt. Taylor made a special trip to England and took samples of the sand with him. Here he received his temporary setback, as the analysis indicated the sand was good only for pottery manufacture and did not possess the required high qualities (silica) necessary for glass manufacture. While this news held up construction for a time, the officials of the first plant were nevertheless determined to go through with their original plans and later met the situation with the use of imported sand. Indecision . . . at this stage may well have ended the venture—and Wallaceburg today would be just another country village. . . .

As the most important part of a glass factory is the "Tank" wherein the glass is made, and from which the molten substance is taken to be moulded (and blown) into the desired article, a search was made for experts in this particular work.

The history and experience connected with the making of the first furnace are very interesting and are not soon forgotten, especially by the oldtimers as a few still employed proudly relate. . . .

A tank engineer from Indiana was recommended as being well qualified in the designing and erection of tanks and the local management engaged his services to build the first such unit at the new plant. The villagers were greatly interested in the operations. . . . It is said that the engineer was "dined, wined and paraded through the streets . . . to mark the beginning of Wallaceburg as the Glass Town."

Methods of preparing the fire clay for the Tank blocks were strangely different from modern practices. Shallow vats of lumber were made, with poles waist high for the workers' support. [The] Clay mixture was placed in the vats, and men with trousers legs rolled up used their bare feet to tramp the clay into its desired consistency. The process, arduous and lengthy, called for other men to mould the clay-mass into various shapes and sizes, following which they were placed beside huge heating stoves until much of the moisture was dried out. These clay shapes— rectangular in form—were still green when erected into the furnace and the actual "burning" of them was accomplished by heat from wood fires lighted at different points inside the furnace. It was Capt. Steinhoff who climbed in the opening of the first furnace and struck the match that started the first such fires. Much interest developed in the days that followed as the furnace was being heated and charged with batch materials, but all were doomed to bitter disappointment when the Tank failed—before production had started.*

---

*Although this particular setback was not experienced by all Canadians attempting the establishment of a glass house, it illustrates the difficulties encountered by nineteenth century glass manufacturers.

. . . No time was lost, however, as another engineer with better experience and methods was soon placed on the job of erecting a second tank. Following a series of setbacks and difficulties, the second tank proved satisfactory and soon the art of making glassware got underway—this was in 1894—about a year following the start of plant construction. It was truly an eventful year. . . .

And then came the gold rush of glass blowers from all parts of North America in hopes of securing employment in the new industry. All work was of a hand-blown and pressed character, because these were the days of artistic accomplishment and trade pride in which workers vied with each other in turning out beautiful ware. Even in those early years of the industry the works of the glass-workers were always greatly admired by many. . . .

The furnaces with their fiery mouths, the rough dark wood of the water troughs and heavy benches, the heavy iron moulds that looked like rough hewn ornaments, even the lighting—orange from the intense fires and blue from the competing daylight—provided a fitting background for the many characters on this vast industrial stage.

Around this first glass producing tank, artisans moved carefully and yet casually with their long fire-tipped rods as they dealt familiarly with the most terrifying elements. At the tip of these long pipes they carried fiery balls of glass which they rolled, pressed and cajoled. . . . Though the heat was . . . terrific . . . some of these veterans . . . would say "it has a nip". . . . .

Increase in production in order to meet demands for more glass-ware led to a gradual mechanization of the industry. The late D. A. Gordon, who held a large interest in the plant, was among those who introduced the first means . . . This method has increased the output, making the Wallaceburg plant one of the major glassware producers in Canada.

Then followed the construction of a continuous tank and a day tank. While this work was under way one of the engineers engaged in this extension to the glass plant lost his life in a disastrous fire in the hotel. . . .

The first two furnaces in the plant, therefore, were of the continuous type, the third was a day furnace and the fourth was a ten-pot furnace. In the early days the factory was of frame construction, but after its first disastrous fire in 1900 the new part was made of brick. There were two other fires. . . .

Capt. J. W. Steinhoff was the firm's first president, with A. C. Laird as secretary and office manager, and John Scott as the managing director. Later D. A. Gordon was named managing director. . . .

The plant was incorporated as the Sydenham Glass Company. . . .

In 1913 an important step took place when the Sydenham Glass Co. became amalgamated with the Diamond Glass Co., which had factories in Montreal, Hamilton and Toronto. This amalgamation was incorporated under the name of Dominion Glass Co., Limited. Sir Charles Gordon was thereupon appointed the first president of the company and continued in this . . . office until his death in 1939.

Henry Herdt was the first general manager of the new firm and was followed by A. H. Grier, J. W. King and Thomas W. Bassett. . . .

Not long after the turn of the century, T. B. Dundas . . . was named secretary and office manager following the resignation of Mr. Laird. Later Mr. Dundas became manager of the plant. Following the amalgamation he was transferred to the head office in Montreal. . . .

Donald Gordon, now deceased, was another local boy who served as manager . . . ; later he was promoted to . . . the head office. T. W. Bassett assumed management in 1925. . . .

From its humble beginnings . . . it has progressed . . . until today it is recognized as being the producer of the largest variety of glassware on the continent. At the present time it employs about 1,000 men and women.

According to oral information, the commercial output of the pre-twentieth century Sydenham Glass Company consisted of chimneys, containers (both bottles and jars) and goblets listed as tablewares.

### AUTHENTICATED SPECIMENS

As is the case with many of the late nineteenth century glass houses, it is impossible to excavate on the site of the original works at Wallaceburg. We have had the good fortune, however, to have interviews with Mr. Davies, the present manager; a glass blower who worked at Wallaceburg in 1898; a lady for whom a glass paperweight was made *circa* 1899; a reliable person whose attribution is accepted by us; and a gentleman, Mr. A. E. W. Kimmerly, whose visit to Wallaceburg was the occasion of the making of a late but special paperweight. Thanks to these sources we have some data relative to this plant's early production, the personnel, and the types of paperweights made for presentation purposes. In addition, there is the splendid gift made by Mr. Davies—the two blow pipes illustrated on Plate 29.

No. 29. Paperweight (by unknown maker). Wallaceburg, (*Circa* 1899). Paperweight (doorstop size). Wallaceburg, 1912. Late Nineteenth-century Blow Pipes from the Old Sydenham Glass Factory, Wallaceburg.

The earliest specimen of Wallaceburg glass in our Collection is a *glass paperweight* 1½" in height and 2¾" in diameter. It has the usual paperweight shape, with a roughly circular opal glass field of a shade of blue authenticated as having been manufactured in the Burlington works. On this field is written—in pencil—the name "Emma." The ground, consisting of well-melted chips of glass coloured red, white and blue with the white predominating, measure 1¾". The whole suggests a Burlington make, but the colour of glass forming the case or body has never been associated with the glass companies of Hamilton, Montreal or other Canadian cities. According to Mr. George Gardiner, who was sent to Wallaceburg from the Burlington Glass Works, the late nineteenth century type of glass manufactured at Wallaceburg was somewhat cloudy. (See Introduction for the causes of "cloudy" glass.) This statement, along with the knowledge that some of the glass blowers came from the Burlington works, where the production of blue opal glass has been established by excavation, suggests that the attribution of this weight is not without reason.

The second *glass paperweight*, an item known to have been produced at the Wallaceburg works, has a particular interest. This weight illustrates the statement previously made that master craftsmen in the art of blowing glass had their followers or pupils, and that these carried on the techniques originated by their masters. This glass paperweight, obtained from a resident of Wallaceburg, was made *circa* 1899. Its full story is as follows: In answer to an advertisement placed in the Wallaceburg newspaper, we received a letter stating that the writer had several old glass paperweights. "The one is a very pretty personal one, given to me when a baby by my uncle who was a glass blower at the Dominion Glass Company at Wallaceburg, Ont. It is sixty years old (in 1957) and in perfect condition." We acquired the weight on condition that we add it to The Edith Chown Pierce and Gerald Stevens Collection in the Royal Ontario Museum. We were pleased and surprised to discover that the weight was one made by a pupil of George Mullin (for a history of Mr. Mullin see chapter 3). This weight is 2⅜" in height and 3½" in diameter. The legend "To Annie" is lettered in cobalt blue on a strip of milk white opal glass. The techniques used in making this weight correspond in every way to those used by Mr. Mullin: the four mushroom-like groups of coloured chips; the milk glass (opal) strip with lettering resembling that used by Mullin; the clear (flint) glass body; and the scar of the pontil rod suggesting a non-commercial piece. The following data are supplied by Mrs. Dickenson of Wallaceburg, for whom the weight was made: maiden name—Annie St. Clair Campbell; uncle's name—Mr. Chester Jorrey; married name—Mrs. John Everett Dickenson.

The third *glass paperweight* was acquired through the kind of good luck that sometimes attends the avid researcher. The complete story of this weight would cover several pages, but it centres about a visit by a Mr. Kimmerly to Wallaceburg in 1912. Mr. Kimmerly arrived in Toronto, and several days later took train for Wallaceburg. Just a few miles from Wallaceburg, the train suddenly braked to a stop. The engineer had noted a body lying beside the tracks. On investigation, the body appeared to be without identification other than a tattoo mark. While in Wallaceburg Mr. Kimmerly became associated with the local Masonic Lodge, and as a souvenir of the occasion a glass blower employed by the Wallaceburg works made him a personal glass paperweight. This weight suggests those made in Hamilton by Mr. "Nix" Daly, a glass blower who produced glass weights of a size suitable for doorstops, but it is an authentic specimen made in the Wallaceburg works in 1912. The clear (flint) glass body measures 3″ in height, and has a circumference of 12″. It contains a milk glass field rectangular in shape inscribed with the letters A. E. W. K. and the date 1912. In addition to these is the insignia of the Masonic Order and four air bubbles forming four flower-like decorations terminating in two red and two yellow sprays. Serving as a ground or base is a typically Canadian collection of coloured chips consisting of finely-ground well-melted bits obtained from sticks passed along from blower to blower in the closing decades of the nineteenth century. The ground in this particular piece consists of chips coloured red, white and blue. The letters stand for Alfred Earl Wyllie Kimmerly.

The subsequent history of the body found on the tracks illustrates the strength of one of Canada's earliest labour unions, the Glass Bottle Blowers' Association of the United States and Canada. According to Mr. Kimmerly, the victim of the accident was interred as a "hobo," but later identification established by the tattoo mark caused the Association of Glass Bottle Blowers to re-inter him with special honours, including a special service attended by many glass workers from Toronto, Hamilton and other centres. Canadian glass workers were a close-knit fraternity!

# 2 *The Glass Houses of Quebec*

(Lower Canada—Quebec)

# 2 *The Glass Houses of Quebec*

## 8. THE GLASS FACTORIES OF THE SEIGNIORY OF VAUDREUIL
### (*circa* 1847—*post* 1875)

THAT PORTION of what is now the province of Quebec that was listed on eighteenth century maps and in nineteenth century directories as the Seigniory de Vaudreuil covers an area extending northward and westward from the confluence of the St. Lawrence and the Ottawa Rivers. Within this area is a settlement having the modern postal address of Hudson, P.Q., covering the village of Hudson, the more modern Hudson Heights and the parish of Vaudreuil. The location is a pleasant one, bordering on the western shore of that widening of the Ottawa River known as The Lake of Two Mountains. On the other shore of the lake are an Indian reserve and the far-famed monastery of Oka. The Indian reserve has a splendid sandy beach. Was it this beach with its white sand that first attracted Quebec glass-makers? Or was it the small sandy coves along the west shore? At any rate, we know that glass was first manufactured in this area *circa* 1846-1847.

Our first source of information about glass-making at Hudson is the directories published in the nineteenth century. The directory, like every printed record, is subject to typographical and other errors. Nevertheless, it can be counted on to supply a lead worthy of investigation. The second source of information was Mrs. Gene Foss of Montreal. Mrs. Foss had investigated the site of one of the Hudson glass houses and had obtained many shards of both coloured and clear glass, some bearing designs.   It is to be regretted that Mrs. Foss lost sight of these shards, but though disappointed, we were pleased to learn that she refused to comment on them in the absence of proof.   The third source was the Rev. E. C. Royle, S.Th., of St. James, Hudson Heights, and St. Mary's, Como, parish of Vaudreuil.   Mr. Royle has been most kind and helpful, and has supplied both oral and documentary data: The latter came from Mr. Royle's *History of the Anglican Parish of Vaudreuil, Hudson Heights, Quebec.*   The fourth source was a letter received from Mr. E. G. Davies, manager of the Wallaceburg branch of the Dominion Glass Company Limited.   Mr. Davies' letter contained a copy of a letter written to him by the late Mr. Joseph Jones, a glass blower working in Canada from 1879.   The fifth source was Mr. L. Seguin, a local historian of note.

The following are excerpts from the present writer's book *The Canadian Collector*:

The first listings found by the writer are contained in an 1857 directory.   This lists; Ottawa Glass Works, C.E. [Canada East-Quebec]. A village in the Seigniory of Vaudreuil.   A large business is carried on here in the manufacture of glass.

Further on in the same directory (in the v's) we find listed the British American Glass Works, Henry W. Jones & Co., proprietors, at Pointe a Cavagnol, Vaudreuil, C. E.

Apparently we have two glass houses, but *Harper's Statistical Gazetteer*, published in the same year, lists only one glass house, and this under "Vaudreuil County."   Further confusion arises when we find in John Lovell's *Chronology of Montreal and Canada* for the year 1893 (and covering the period 1752-1925) that "Desbarats & Derbishire start a glass factory at Vaudreuil, A.D. 1847," and also, "The Montreal Glass Co., at Hudson, makes chimneys, bottles and insulators, A.D. 1866."   [The insulators herein mentioned were those used for telegraph lines.   The early type, made by many glass houses, may be distinguished by several features including the use of a medium-deep aquamarine-coloured glass.]

The problem is (partially) solved when in an 1871 directory we find listed, "Canada Glass Works Co., Ltd., Hudson.   Hudson formerly called Pointe a Cavagnol."

Thus we find that the Vaudreuil referred to is the county and not the village, and that "Ottawa Glass Works, C.E." was a postal address used by the glass works established by Desbarats and Derbishire in 1847 because of its distance from the village of Vaudreuil.

Lovell's *Gazetteer of British North America* for the year 1874 lists "Hudson, or Pointe a Cavagnol.   It contains a glass factory."

*The Canadian Collector* further lists the following names and dates of the several glass companies operating in this area, obtained from directories, etc.:

> Ottawa Glass Works, *circa* 1847
> British American Glass Works, *circa* 1855
> Montreal Glass Company, *circa* 1866
> Canada Glass Works Co. Ltd., *circa* 1871

The following are excerpts from, first, Mr. Royle's *History* and, secondly, a letter received from Mr. Royle in March, 1959:

The *History* (page 92) reads:

About this time (1847) the village of Como received its present name. Mr. Shepherd [a gentleman whose Memoir supplied Mr. Royle with data relative to the area] notes that when the Ottawa Glass Works was established in the Pointe Cavagnol district in 1847, the Post Office took the company name—Ottawa Glass Works Post Office. A natural result of this was a great confusion in the mails; a lot of the mail for Pointe Cavagnol went up to Ottawa. . . . Mr. Shepherd says: "I saw Mr. King, the Inspector, on the subject. . . . After a time it struck me that 'Como' would be very suitable, as it was situated on a very beautiful lake, perhaps not equal to the one in Italy, nevertheless it was decided to call the Post Office 'Como'. . . ."

For some years the manufacture of glass played an important part in the economy of the district. First established by Mr. Desjardins on the little hill where the Johnson farm and properties now stand (1955), they operated for several years. [The author feels that Mr. Desbarats, the Montreal printer, should be credited rather than Mr. Desjardins—a matter of opinion.] Mr. Matthews opened The Canada Glass Works in Hudson just to the west of the Wilson ice house on the Nesbit property; and a third operated on the site of the present Como saw mill (Hodgson Bros.). The two factories at Como led to the establishment of quite a large settlement, and the glassblowers were very highly paid for the times—five dollars a day. . . . Several families came to Como from the States. This made Como the largest centre of the district; the present village of Hudson at that time consisted of only three or four farms. . . . With the end of the Civil War in the United States, the Americans exported a flood of cheap glass to Canada and the Como glass works all closed. The glass blowers went back to the United States (?) with the exception of Thomas Hommel. His daughter, Mrs. F. Davis, is still living in Como. The factory in Hudson carried on for several years.

[Note: The author has visited Mrs. Davis (1957) and obtained the information that her father blew bottles of a type and kind unknown to Mrs. Davis.]

The letter mentioned previously in the text contains this additional information:

The factory in Hudson, Quebec, known as the Canada Glass Works, stood on the edge of the Lake of Two Mountains, close to the existing government wharf. A local resident remembers that by 1891 this building had fallen into total ruin. Then apparently it was repaired and used as summer cottages for some years, being finally destroyed by fire at an unknown date. The site of the factory building itself is now completely covered.

This area might have had the same type of commercial success enjoyed by the town of Wallaceburg, Ontario, if the local people and financial interests had persevered.

The letter written to Mr. Davies by Mr. Jones throws little light on the Vaudreuil glass houses, but is is worthy of mention. An excerpt from this letter reads:

Now as to Hudson, I do not know very much. I must have been only about twelve years old when I first heard about it while yet in New Jersey.* It then must have been closed down quite a while before that. The only thing I can say is there must have been a factory there, for while on a fishing trip up the Ottawa River we camped on an island opposite Hudson, and were shown the place where the factory was. There was no building, only the places in the ground, which no doubt were the caves and foundations for ovens and buildings. As to who owned or operated it I never found out, only they made nothing but bottles the old way, that is by cast ring. This I heard from a few blowers I met, who had worked there.

---

*This reference to New Jersey, and the knowledge that Mr. Jones was later to move to Canada where he blew glass, is of some importance. The reason for this is that some specimens of glass produced in the early New Jersey glass houses, as well as pieces manufactured in the Northern New York State houses of Redford and Redwood, resemble authenticated specimens known to have been made in the Mallorytown glass works. It would be interesting to learn the origin of these similar forms. For the present, could we say that United Empire Loyalist glass blowers, learning their trade in the glass houses of New Jersey and migrating to Canada, carried the techniques of trailed handles, threaded necks and crude doorstops to a new country?

Possibly the best documented data on the earliest period of glass manufacture in the area is that supplied by Mr. L. Seguin, in a series of articles published in the newspaper *La Presqu'ile* during the month of August, 1956. This series is headed "Vaudreuil Heights Glass Industry" (by Robert-Lionel Seguin), and begins:

In the middle of the last century, a great industrial awakening took place in the Vaudreuil and Rigaud seigniories. It was at first a glass industry: . . . the glass factory . . . was situated a bit west of Pointe-Cavagnol.

This series of articles was written in French. We do not attempt to translate Mr. Seguin's history in full, but only such excerpts as are of value to those interested in Canadian glass rather than those interested in the history of Vaudreuil, Como, Hudson and the district in general. The sources supplied by Mr. Seguin appear to be impeccable, as they consist mainly of records on deposit in the Judiciary Archives of Montreal.

The initial move to establish a glass house in the Pointe Cavagnol area took place on September 24, 1845. On that day Messrs. D. Masson, Jules-Edouard Brady, F. Coste and F.-X. Desjardins, the last from Pointe Cavagnol, met to form an association. The firm of Masson and Company proposed to undertake "the construction of buildings, furnaces (and) the mixing of the materials which enter into the making of glass. . . ." This was left to the discretion of Mr. François Coste. The proposed location of the glass house was "lot no. 19 of the concession above Pointe Cavagnol."

The usual practice in attempting to manufacture glass in North America was to issue shares and obtain capital, and only then to begin the erection of buildings and furnaces. Control frequently changed hands, and shares were shuffled back and forth. The career of Masson and Company was no exception to the general rule. Mr. Seguin wrote:

The company continued to falter until March 9, 1847, when Damase Masson and Jean-Baptiste Beaudry . . . sold to Stewart Derbishire . . . all their rights "in buildings, lot and other assets forming and composing the establishment for the exploitation of a glass works, the whole being located on the lot attached to a farm belonging to Francois-Xavier Desjardins situated and located in Vaudreuil." The vendors also gave up "all the articles of smelting to be found in the smelter of Messrs. Brush and Company of Montreal, approximately 500 fire bricks . . . in Lachine, and eight cases of clay, now in the sheds of the customs in St.-Jean."* This was the end of Masson and Company and the first step toward the establishment of the Ottawa Glass Company.

The most significant result of the Masson venture was to prepare the way for a gentleman whose name is well known to students of nineteenth century printing in Canada, Stewart Derbishire. It appears that Mr. Derbishire agreed to pay the sum of £825 over the period of a year and a half, the rate of interest being 6%. Although his financial aid and interest did not result in the actual production of glass, it introduced to the scheme his partner in the printing business, Georges Desbarats of the firm of Desbarats and Derbishire.

Associated with the new firm, the Ottawa Glass Company, were Dr. Louis-Cyrus Macaire and, most important of all, Desbarats. The last of the original members, Jules Brady, surrendered his shares to Derbishire. Mr. Seguin wrote:

Stewart Derbishire gave to Desbarats his share of the glass works along with "all the wood, clay, ashes and other materials, all the horses and animals and all the claims." However, Desbarats had to give to George Watson, merchant of Montreal, shares in the factory to extent of 750 louis. . . .

It was decided . . . to form another company including Frederick Charles Hockmuth, Bastien Hockmuth and George William Hirsh. The first one was of Montreal while the other(s) . . . were glass manufacturers in Vaudreuil.

Mr. Seguin's account continues with the information that the site had remained unchanged, and that it "measured òne arpent and three quarters of frontage (from the Ottawa River to the public road), by three arpents in width."

The manipulations and sales of shares continued, adding new names to the record. Further excerpts of interest are:

*The preceding is important, for it suggests that the clay used was imported rather than a local clay, readily available along the shores of both the Ottawa and St. Lawrence Rivers, which has been proven to be fit for the manufacture of pottery. Have the qualities of clays obtainable in Canada been investigated for uses other than that of pottery?

In 1850 Henry Hockmuth sold all his rights . . . to Frederick Boden. At the same time . . . Bastien Hockmuth and George William Hirsh abandoned to Boden all . . . rights; . . . Boden was now owner . . . Boden became partner with Jean-Baptist Lebert. . . . Desbarats still held shares. . . .

Additional information supplied from this source suggests that the name of one of the master craftsmen employed by this house was John Marks, working "near 1853."

It appears that the third step in the development of the old Masson and Company glass house was that it became the first to produce glass on a scale to compete with houses in St. Johns, Montreal, and Hamilton. Mr. Seguin writes:

The factory kept on expanding. It was in full activity around 1871. So, in the provincial directory of that year, it was mentioned that in Hudson a large business is carried on in the manufacture of glass. The factory remained in operation for a few more years, hiring almost exclusively Anglo-Saxon workers. It started declining after 1875.

We must give Mr. Seguin a great deal of credit for the data on this earliest proven Quebec glass house. Indeed, the list of buildings and equipment included in the sale of Mr. Desbarat's share gives a splendid picture of what this Canadian glass works comprised after years of effort. This listing suggests that it hoped to produce window glass. If it did so, this would be the first authenticated attempt at this type of glass so far recorded in Canada.

A researcher could spend a lifetime in an unsuccessful attempt to document every item produced by a specific glass house. This holds good for each of the several factories located in the seigniory of Vaudreuil. As this writer does not pretend to have all the answers to questions pertaining to Canadian glass, he can only supply such data as have been checked and cross-checked. To do this we have interviewed the Rev. Mr. Royle, Mr. Seguin, Mrs. Davis, Mr. Davies (who is himself interested in Vaudreuil and the history of glass in Canada in general) and several of the local residents. The net result is small compared to that obtained at Hamilton, Ontario, but some additional hints as to items of a type known as "collectors' " have been gathered.

No. 30.   Specimens attributed to the glass houses of Vaudreuil
(Attributions based on data obtained in the area.)

The proven data may be summarized as follows: There were two glass houses located in the Hudson-Como area, and these two houses were known by five or more names.   The difficulty is that through the years confusion has arisen as to specific sites and names.   We think it best to number the sites, number one being that located in Hudson and fronting on the Lake of Two Mountains (Ottawa River), and number two that situated at Como.   Our reconstruction may be incorrect, but it must be remembered that we have two sites and five names, and much confusion still exists.

According to such sources as directories, the Ottawa Glass Works (Masson and Company, later the Canada Glass Works Co. Ltd.) attempted window glass, bottles, containers and lighting equipment.   The British American Glass Works, later the Montreal Glass Company, made chimneys, bottles and insulators.

The one clear piece of local evidence about special pieces came from Mrs. Davis, who claimed that her husband had made them to take home. We are sorry that Mrs. Davis could not remember specific types, nor could she produce such items. Nevertheless, it seems certain that one lighting equipment was produced by one of these glass houses. The reason for this is that great numbers of this type of hand-lamp have been found in the province of Quebec, from Montreal east to Quebec city, and that this type is rarely discovered in Ontario. Two identical specimens were acquired, both obtained in the Hudson area and claimed as local products. Although both lamps were made in the same mould or a copy thereof, the one was made from a glass coloured a deep amber and the other from a clear flint.

In addition to these lamps there are other types of glass said to have been made in the area, although proof is lacking. Covered sugar bowls in deep amber glass as well as "raw glass" paperweights containing a cross are said to be owned by local families.

Published materials yield some additional information about the early days of glass-making in Quebec, and in particular about the Vaudreuil factories. For example, a report dated 1868 and entitled *Statements relating to Trade, Navigation, Mining, etc., etc., etc., of the Dominion of Canada; and Annual Report on the Commerce of Montreal for 1867\** gives under the heading "Glass and Glass-Works" data relating to imported glass and glasswares, and supplied the information that the word "Glass" in official reports represents "Window Glass." The statement:

The manufacture of glassware in Canada during the past two years has reduced the imported article from 50 per cent in the average of the five years above mentioned [1853 through 1857], to 41.26 per cent in 1865-1866, the ratios being: value of Window Glass imported, $201,405, Glass manufactures, about $141,472. The ratios in 1866-1867 were: imported Window Glass, $278,662, Glass manufactures, say $183,412, or 39.69 per cent. of the whole imports. The opinion has been expressed that the consumption of all kinds of Glass and Glassware by the population of the Dominion (nearly 4,000,000) would give employment to twenty-five glass furnaces, in producing the multitudinous articles now in daily use among all classes of the community, and giving steady remunerative

---

\*Fifth publication, by Wm. J. Patterson, Secretary Board of Trade, and Corn Exchange Association, Montreal, Starke & Co., Commercial Printers, St. Francois Xavier Street, p. 60.

employment to hundreds of persons.   The constituents of Green Glass
(except Soda-Ash, which would have to be imported) are abundant; and all
the requisites for the production of Flint Glass may be said to be at hand.
    The Customs duty on Glass and Glassware is 15 per cent. . . .
    *Glass Works.*   There are no particulars at hand respecting the Glass
Works at Hamilton, in Ontario. . . .*
    The Canada Glass Co.'s Works at Hudson, Province of Quebec, have
been established for several years.   The operations, which at first were
limited to the manufacture of Druggist's Bottles, Telegraph Insulators,
etc., have been recently much extended.   The first addition made to the
articles produced at the works consisted chiefly of Chimneys and other
Lamp-ware.   The capital has been increased by the sum of $10,000; a
steam-engine has been erected to drive all the machinery, which includes
a Crushing-mill, &c.; and the manufacture of German Flint Glass is now
carried on.   The consumption of raw material at the Hudson Works in
1867 included,—180,000 lbs. of Soda-Ash, 3,500 lbs. of Saltpetre, 5,000
lbs. Red Lead, 4,000 lbs. of Borax, and smaller quantities of chemicals
for colouring.   About 100,000 lbs. of Lime, and 360,000 lbs. of Sand
(from the Co's own property in neighbourhood of the works),—and the
value of the Glass produced was $56,000.

Another publication, *Products and Manufactures of the New Dominion*
(by H. Beaumont Small, S.C.L., Ottawa, George E. Desbarats, Printer
and Publisher, 1868) contains a great deal of glass-making information.
This is mostly relative to the St. Lawrence Glass Company of Montreal,
but the following reference is to the Hudson glass house:

There is another establishment in operation at Hudson on the Ottawa
River, where the coarser kinds of bottles, telegraph insulators, &c., are
manufactured; and these two, the pioneers of this useful article of commerce, will doubtless soon be followed by others in various parts of the
Dominion.†

There are a number of additional references to be found, but in the
main these duplicate such data as are contained in this text.

---

*This remark is typical of the times.   Prior to Confederation, and for several years after,
official reports emanating from Toronto and Montreal did not take into consideration such commercial activities as were in actual production in other than their own sections, a practice that
has caused much trouble and confusion to researchers.
    †This last supports the writer's assertion that statisticians in Montreal, even when their
work was printed in Upper Canada, were unaware of or ignored the products of Upper Canada.
At the time this reference to Quebec glass houses was being written the Hamilton Glass Co.
was in production; and as for "pioneers," the Mallorytown Glass Works antedated all herein
listed.

### 9. JOHN C. SPENCE, MONTREAL (1854-1867)

IT IS QUITE possible that both French and English Canada can boast of a glass stainer antedating John C. Spence, but until such time as an earlier artist in glass is proven to have worked here he must be regarded as the pioneer in this field of Canadian endeavour. John Spence was the only representative of glass-making in Canada chosen to exhibit at the Universal Exhibition of 1855 at Paris. Several persons interested in the story of Canadian glass have questioned the statement that Mr. Spence made glass and hold to the opinion that he merely obtained sheet glass from other sources and coloured and stained it to order. The author holds that this claim is refuted by the official report of the items representing Canada at the above mentioned exhibition.

A detailed account of Mr. Spence's activities has yet to be written. This writer's interest in this earliest of Montreal's glass makers was aroused by the late Mr. Harry A. Norton, one of Canada's most noted collectors of early glass. Mr. Norton, whose contributions to the Montreal Museum of Fine Arts we have noted in the introduction, travelled the world searching for interesting and historic specimens of the glass-maker's art, and was ready to acquire any specimen of particular interest. The writer obtained from Mr. Norton several items which he said had been made about 1850 in a glass works on Notre Dame St. in Montreal. We regret that we did not obtain the source from which Mr. Norton had acquired these items; but we do know that he was most careful, and that he had a well-earned reputation as a collector of authentic specimens.

The first official recognition of Mr. Spence's work is found in *Canada at the Universal Exhibition of 1855* (Toronto, John Lovell, 1856; printed by order of the Legislative Assembly). This is a splendid reference source, a giant project for the time and possibly the best of its kind ever compiled in Canada. It lists exhibits and exhibitors, and includes almost every category of arts and crafts exemplified in the Canada of that day, from axes to glass, from works of art like oil paintings by Paul Kane to fancy work by Indians. The only name associated with glass is that of Mr.

Spence, though we know that glass was being made in the Vaudreuil area. Each category was listed as a "class," and Mr. Spence was represented in two classes, 18 and 24.

Class Eighteen (Glass and Pottery) contains one entry: "No. 327, Spence (J.C.), Montreal, Lower Canada: Stained Glass." A description of this entry is not given, nor did it appear to be worthy of special mention in the report.

Class Twenty-four (Furniture and Decoration, Section 4) lists "No. 354, Spence (J.C.), Montreal, Lower Canada: Work Table of glass, Painted and Gilded." In contrast to the first, this exciting entry apparently aroused great interest, as it was acquired and later sent to Sydenham Palace, England, where it helped to form the nucleus of a permanent Canadiana exhibit.

It is to be regretted that the report did not illustrate any of the pieces. It would be most interesting to have some idea of the techniques used by Mr. Spence to produce a table of glass worthy of being placed on public view in Sydenham Palace.

The second interesting bit of documentation is an advertisement in the *Canada Directory* for 1857-1858. On page 414, under the S's, we find "Spence, J. C., manufacturer of stained, embossed, and figured enamelled glass, &c., Canada stained glass works, 21 Notre Dame St." A half-page advertisement on page 1262 gives a much more complete picture of Mr. Spence's abilities, however. It reads:

Canada Stained & Ornamental Glass Works—No. 21, Notre Dame Street (Near Donegana Hotel), Montreal. John C. Spence, Manufacturer of every Description of Stained, Painted, Embossed, Cut and figured Enamelled Glass, For Windows of Churches, Public Buildings, Hotels, Steamboats, Offices, Halls, Staircases, Side and Panel Lights, Figures, Coats of Arms, Monograms, Landscapes, Flowers, Borders, Rosettes, executed to any design. Leaded Windows in Cathedrals and Ground Glass for Churches, &c, &c. Signal Glasses for Railway and Steamboat Signals, Hollow and Solid Lenses, Bent Hand Lamp Glasses, &c. &c. Gilding and Writing on Glass, Glass Signs, Druggists' Show Jars with Coats of Arms, Tablets, Glass Labels, &c. Red, Blue, Green, Purple, Orange and Yellow Glass, in Sheets, or Cut to Sizes. Lantern Frames and Glass for Hotels, Saloons, Halls, &c. Designs and Estimates forwarded on application. Specimens may be seen at the Office. (Montreal, October, 1857).

It is an impressive advertisement.

Mr. Spence continued to be listed in Montreal directories for a number of years, but appears to have encountered little success as a maker of glass and to have contented himself finally with glass staining. This resulted in his becoming associated with a Mr. John McArthur. The *Montreal Directory* for 1860-1861 lists "Spence, John C., (of McArthur & Spence) house 67 Alexander." Under the firm name we find, "MCARTHUR & SPENCE, plain and ornamental painters, glass stainers, &c., 118 McGill, cor. of Commissioners Square."

*Mackay's Montreal Directory*, 1862-1863, suggests that Mr. Spence and Mr. McArthur agreed to disagree. This work lists "Spence, John C., glass stainer, &c., 52 Great St. James, house 67 Alexander," and "McArthur, John, (of John McArthur & Son,) house 3 Abbotsford terrace, 540 St. Catherine near Drummond."

Mr. Spence appears to have carried on as a stainer of glass for many more years, and it would be interesting to attempt to trace such stained glass windows of his design as are extant.

## AUTHENTICATED SPECIMENS

The several items attributed to Mr. Spence that are now in either The Edith Chown Pierce and Gerald Stevens Collection of Early Canadian Glass in the Royal Ontario Museum or the author's personal collection, consist of those small glass containers known as vigil lights. Those in the Royal Ontario Museum were obtained from Mr. Norton in trade for water colour paintings by Paul Caron, the Montreal artist. Mr. Norton, being a wealthy man, would not sell the vigil lights but, knowing our interest in things Canadian, agreed to the exchange. Those in the author's collection were purchased in and about Montreal. For the information of those not conversant with them, vigil lights are small glass containers used to hold burning candles, usually measuring about 3″ in height by 2″ in diameter. The original use may or may not have been religious, but these little cups have for centuries held candles lighted as offerings of devotion and placed before pictures or statues in Catholic

No. 31.   Four Vigil Lights, attributed to the Canada Stained & Ornamental Glass Works (John C. Spence) Montreal.   Colours: deep blue, pale amber, deep blue, olive, green. (*Circa* 1855).   (*Centre*) Lamp: deep amber: applied handle: ribbed pattern.   Made at the Canada Glass Works, Hudson (Vaudreuil) (*Circa* 1870).

churches.   Vigil lights were also used for many years to decorate Christmas trees or gardens used for nighttime entertainment, and on other occasions calling for out-of-doors illumination before the introduction of later types of lighting.   Indeed, an old-time blown glass vigil light seems to have an aura of devotion or romance.

Although vigil lights are difficult to authenticate, the combination of circumstances resulting in the attribution of these specimens leaves little doubt as to their authenticity.   This is not the writer's opinion alone, but is based on discussion with several glass authorities in both Canada and the United States.   The obvious reasons are the source from which the specimens were obtained, the techniques used in manufacture, the fact that both the city of Montreal and the Province of Quebec as a whole are predominantly Roman Catholic and that Catholic churches there still use vast numbers of vigil lights.   The specimens herein listed are either free-blown or blown-moulded.

A *pale or honey amber light*, 3¼″ in height and 2½″ in diameter at the opening, circular and slightly bulbous.   This was blown in a partial mould, then expanded and shaped and, by use of a pontil rod finished off with a folded rim.   The mould had a ribbed design.

A *dark olive green light*, 3″ in height and $2\frac{7}{16}$″ in diameter. The technique used in manufacture is similar to that of the amber specimen.

A *royal blue light*, 3″ in height and $2\frac{5}{8}$″ in width including the collar. It is free blown, and has a plain rim at right angles to the body. The body of this piece is plain, and does not have the ribbed design and bulbous shape of the preceding items.

All three specimens show the scar indicating the use of a pontil rod.

The two specimens in the author's collection are very similar to nos. 1 and 2. One has the usual ribbed design, but is of opal glass. The second has a mould blown diamond pattern and is royal blue in colour.

## 10. THE FOSTER BROTHERS GLASS WORKS, ST. JOHNS (1855-1880)

PRIOR TO the year 1855 three brothers migrated from the neighbourhood of Boston, Mass., to the town of St. Johns, Lower Canada, and there erected a glass works. The number three may be somewhat arbitrary, as two different but very reliable sources give respectively two names and one. It may have been that two Foster brothers, George and Henry, established the glass works, and that the third, Charles, carried on until the St. Johns works were closed and the equipment moved to Montreal.

The record of this glass house begins with a listing in the *Canada Directory* for 1857-1858. Under the F's in the St. Johns section we find "Foster Brothers, glass manufacturers, Albert St." In an attempt to discover what articles and types of wares were made in this plant, we visited St. Johns, made inquiries, and were fortunate enough to learn that there was a lady living in the town whose grandmother had been a Miss Foster. We called on the lady, a Mrs. William Campbell, were shown four goblets and a covered bottle made in the Foster Brothers glass house, and obtained valuable information relating to a Canadian glass house that went out of operation eighty years ago. We acquired two of the goblets and the covered bottle, and studied the two remaining goblets.

According to Mrs. Campbell, the Foster brothers had moved to St. Johns because of the opportunities offered in a Canada badly in need of glass manufacturers. The reason for their settling in St. Johns is not known.   But it is possible that the apparent success of the pottery located there, Farrar & Soule, suggested that St. Johns would become a manufacturing centre with large outlets in the nearby city of Montreal.   Be that as it may, the brothers erected their glass house and began production.

The Fosters continued in business until 1880, when Mr. Charles Foster, the then manager appears, as representative of the family, to have sold the Foster interests to Messrs. William and David Yuile.   The exact date of this transaction is not known, but it occurred not earlier than shortly before December, 1879, and not later than 1880, when this plant was closed for all time.

The second source of information was supplied by Mr. Davies, of the Wallaceburg branch of the Dominion Glass Company Limited.   In his search for information relative to glass-making in Canada, Mr. Davies had written to the late Mr. "Joe" Jones, glass blower.   Mr. Jones replied with a letter describing the beginnings of successful glass manufacture in the Province of Quebec.

The following is a quotation from Mr. Jones' letter:

It was the early part of December 1879 that my Father moved from Glassboro, N.J. to St. Johns, Que.   I was then 15 years old, and of course went to work in the factory.   It was at that time operated by the Yuile Bros. (William and David) who had taken over the plant from a person by name Charles Foster who built the tank (?), and it was known as the Foster Tank, and consisted of nine ring holes.   There were four cast ring shops, two insulator presses (the old hand press style) and three glory hole shops, of which I carried in on two of them.   It was there I met some blowers who at some time had worked at Hudson, and I believe they learned to blow there as their relatives, the old folks, were on farms there, and these men were the descendants.   The plant at St. Johns was managed by a man by name William Borland, and the office clerk was an Ed. Sawyer.   I must say two nice fellows and all liked them.   The boss packer was a man by name John Farnham.   The working staff was from the States, South Jersey; and a couple who at one time worked at Hudson.

Mr. Jones's letter continues with much data relative to Montreal glass houses, but one further mention of St. Johns is of importance: "At St. Johns it (the Company) was known as The Excelsior Glass Company."

Although the data relative to the St. Johns glass works are somewhat meagre we have, thanks to Mrs. Campbell, Mr. Davies and Mr. Jones, managed to ascertain the approximate dates of this house and several types of glass made there. Thanks must also be extended to Mr. Charles P. de Volpi of Montreal, who was instrumental in our acquiring the *embossed bottle* which will be noted in the listing of authenticated items.

A glass house operating in Canada *circa* 1855 would of course produce containers of several kinds. That the St. Johns house did so is proven by the acquisition of a *bottle* (that obtained from Mr. de Volpi) which is embossed "Foster Brothers St. Johns C.E." This bottle is gourd-shaped, with a pointed bottom. The metal is heavy, and of a medium-deep aquamarine colour. The stopper, now missing, would have been of glass held in place by metal wire. This is a typical bottle of a type used throughout Quebec to hold a French-Canadian soft drink made from spruce chips steeped and strengthened with yeast, and known as spruce beer. This old-time French-Canadian beverage was sold throughout the Province during the nineteenth century and the early decades of the twentieth, and is still obtainable in rural districts. It is a splendid refresher on a hot summer's day and, possibly because of the yeast, needs a bottle with a very tight-fitting top. There was a reason for the peculiar shape of these bottles. It was the custom in Quebec for private citizens to go into business in a small way and to manufacture, and possibly sell from a cart driven through the streets of Montreal, this home-made concoction. These hawkers seldom sold by the bottle, but would pour out a measure into a glass and offer a large salt-shaker to those who wished to have their spruce beer foaming. Thus the glass bottles containing the drink would be taken home and used over and over again. The bottles were stacked in wooden cases partitioned into squares, and there was no need for the bottles to have a flattened base. The Foster bottles tell of a bygone glass house and a bygone age when business did not have the complications of the present time. These bottles measure from 8¾″ to 9¼″ in height and 9¼″ at the greatest circumference. They were blown in a two-piece mould, and finished by means of a snap.

A number of these bottles have been authenticated. Several of them are plain, without the embossed name. All are typical.

Two additional specimens representative of this glass house are in the possession of Mrs. William Campbell. These are *pressed glass goblets* of a basically common type. There is one great difference. These goblets, presented to Mrs. Campbell's mother on her wedding day, show that the Fosters knew how to use the engraving wheel when the occasion arose. These goblets are well engraved with floral designs, and suggest that if a finer wheel was used this glass house could have cut glass. This interesting speculation stems from a blown tumbler which the author acquired in the St. Johns area and which is attributed to this glass house. This tumbler has been shown to Mrs. Campbell and compared with her goblets. Mrs. Campbell feels, as does the author, that the type of glass used to manufacture the tumbler, the type of engraving used to decorate the piece, the simple fluted cutting, and the free blown technique proven by the scar of a pontil rod used in its shaping all suggest a St. Johns origin. This piece is designated as "attributed to."

The two *plain flint glass goblets* obtained from Mrs. Campbell are clear glass goblets made from a non-lead glass using a two-piece mould. They are 6⅛" in height, of a type known to have been made in some numbers. (See Plate 24.)

The *covered bottle* obtained from Mrs. Campbell, and made by Foster Brothers *circa* 1860, is interesting both as an authenticated specimen of early Canadian glass, and as recalling the days when liquids like vinegar, kerosene and oil were sold in bulk, and carried away from the merchant's shop in the customer's own container. To serve this purpose nineteenth century glass manufacturers made stout bottles and protected them with woven covers of many types.

According to Mrs. Campbell, the Foster Brothers grew willow shoots from which to weave covers for glass bottles made in their glass house. Mrs. Campbell says she remembers her parents talking about the plantations of willows from which the covers were woven, and that the women-folk sometimes assisted in this art. The bottle obtained from Mrs. Campbell measures 10" in height and 4¼" in diameter. As far as can be ascertained without removing the cover, it was made in a two-piece mould. The covering is of especially fine workmanship and includes a handle woven into and incorporated with the covering.

## 11. The St. Lawrence Glass Company, Montreal (1867-1875)

WE CAN begin the documentation of this Canadian glass house with an excerpt from a letter supplied by Basil Stuart-Stubbs, formerly reference librarian of the Redpath Library at McGill University. Mr. Stuart-Stubbs wrote:

"The St. Lawrence Glass Works appears for the last time in the volume [*Directory*] for the year 1875-1876. It is probably safe to say that they had stopped operating."

No. 32.   Advertisement in *Products and Manufactures of the New Dominion*,
by H. Beaumont Small.   1868.

The author believes that this is correct, for no one has discovered any proof that the St. Lawrence works carried on at a later date, at least under that name. Thus we have the closing date of this house, but what of the opening? This question is answered in the report, *Statements relating to Trade, Navigation, Mining etc.*, quoted in chapter 8. On page 61 we find the following:

The St. Lawrence Glass Company have established their extensive works in the City of Montreal for the manufacture of Flint Glass. Operations were commenced in the Fall of 1867; it is not, therefore, possible to do more in this notice than to say that they have been projected on a scale abundantly large to meet the growing wants of the Dominion, that they are adapted to produce the finest kinds of pressed and cut Flint Glassware, and that under its enterprising directors and managers the works are likely to be profitable as a pecuniary investment while in every respect they will be creditable to the manufacturing skill and enterprise of Canada.

Although the preceding reads almost like a paid advertisement, it has the merit of giving the opening date and a suggestion of the proposed production. It would be interesting to know just what the term "cut glassware" represented, as a full-page advertisement in another publication suggests that the cutting was limited to lamp shades.

Although there are numbers of references to this glass house, some of which will be listed, the most important is that contained in the 1868 publication, *Products and Manufactures of the New Dominion* (for full title see chapter 8). This prints a full page cut of the buildings comprising this house, and on the reverse of the page a full page advertisement listing a great many products. On pages 143-146 is to be found the following:

Hitherto the glassware of domestic use in the greatest requisition, such as lamp chimneys, goblets and phials, has been imported from Europe and the United States. But to obviate this a large establishment named the St. Lawrence Glass Works has been established and brought into successful operation by Mr. A. McK. Cochrane, of Montreal, under the management of an experienced superintendent. The various processes are carried on in four large brick buildings, forming a quadrangle. As this is a new branch of industry in the Dominion, the following description will prove interesting:

The sand to be used in its manufacture must be the purest white sand that can be obtained; this is brought from Berkshire, Mass., and undergoes first a process of complete drying, after which it is mixed with refined pearlash and other ingredients in certain proportions; it is then filled into pots standing around an intensely hot furnace inside of a wide circular chimney. These pots have each an aperture at the top corresponding with another in the wall of the chimney. Here the pots, to be described hereafter, are speedily brought to a white heat, and their contents melted to a partially fluid consistency. At each pot a glass blower is stationed, forming one of a number of workmen engaged in completing the same article. This group is called *a shop*, and it is seen at the end of each day how much each shop has accomplished.

In making lamp chimneys, the glass blower takes out a sufficient quantity of molten glass from his pot on the end of his long blow-pipe, and blows gently into it. This distends the mass a very little; he then hangs it down and swings it twice to make it elongate by the combined power of gravitation and a gentle centrifugal force, after which he blows again sufficiently to swell the lower part into the shape of a lamp chimney. It is then hard enough to retain its shape, and the blow-pipe with the chimney adhering is carried off by a boy to the finisher, who rolls the pipe as if on a turning lathe, while he performs the operation of cutting off the bottom, and moulding the edge round it, both operations being performed by a long pair of compasses. He applies a circular measure to ascertain that the bottom of the chimney is the right gauge, and after the neck is detached at the proper distance by a clean cut, the glass is carried away on a rod to the *glory-hole*, an aperture in another very hot furnace, where after it has been heated, it is brought back to be finished. A *shop* for the manufacture of lamp chimneys consists of a blower, a finisher, and two boys, and the average daily amount turned out by each *shop* is from sixty to seventy-five dozen according to size.

In the manufacture of phials, a different process is used. The blower takes out enough molten glass on the end of his blow-pipe to make a phial, or rather as in all processes, a little more than enough, and after blowing very slightly into it, he drops it into a mould, which is shut upon it by a boy; he then blows forcibly into it, causing the glass within the mould to expand and fill it exactly, while the remainder of the air rising in the glass above the mould, expands it like a soap bubble which, when he takes away his pipe, explodes with a sharp report. A boy carries away the phials as quickly as made.

In the manufacture of goblets, the molten glass is dropped into the mould in the proper quantity for a goblet; into this mould the pressman forces down a plunger with a strong lever power, and immediately opening it, he brings out a perfect goblet, which is carefully caught by the foot, and carried to the glory-hole, where it is heated. It is then polished

1. A. Cantin's, Marine Works.  Roberts & Reinhold, Lithographers, Place d'Armes, Montreal.  3. Morland, Watson & Co's. Shot Tower.
5. Lachine Road.                                    2                                 4. Lachine Canal.

ST LAWRENCE GLASS WORKS.

No. 33. Pressed Flint Glass "Beaver" and "Exhibition" Goblets, Excelsior Glass Co.,
St. John's, P.Q., 1878-1880. Advertisement in *Products and Manufactures of the New
Dominion*, by H. Beaumont Small. 1868.

by the finisher and carried off to the annealing oven.    This is a long low chamber, with a sort of railway in the bottom, on which trays covered with glassware are shoved or drawn along.    It is exceedingly hot at the end at which they go in, and the heat diminishes gradually towards the end at which they come out, which is very little heated.    As the day's work proceeds, the new trays filled with the wares push the previous ones further along till in about twenty-four hours from the time it went in, each tray comes out.    The ware is then examined, counted, credited to the different shops, and carefully packed in barrels for sale.

The pots alluded to constitute one of the most costly and difficult parts of the process of glass making.    They are of a peculiar shape, measuring about three feet every way, sitting flat on the ground, but circular in every direction, with an opening at the front in the top, covered with a pent roof calash-fashion.    The thickness of these pots is about three inches, made of the purest fire clay, of which (*i.e.* the kind requisite for this purpose) only two or three beds are known to exist, one in England and another in Missouri; but as these bulky and brittle articles are risky to be transported, the St. Lawrence Glass Company means to make its own pots.    There is a peculiarity about this process of pot-making which deserves notice.    The clay, after being properly mixed, has to be trodden by men for weeks in order to knead it to the right consistency; and no ingenuity that has yet been brought to bear on the subject has been able to substitute any other power with equal advantage.

The St. Lawrence Glass Company guarantee a dividend of twelve and a half per cent.

The author feels that this long quotation is worthy of inclusion in this work.    The technical information will not be new to many persons who will read this book but the fact that such data are contained in a Canadian publication of 1868 points up the importance of any contemporary work on Canadian glass.    Is it not strange that nineteenth century Canadian glass appears to have been unknown until the 1950's, when, with the discovery of Mallorytown, everyone appeared to be surprised that Canada had had even one working glass house?

Additional sources are recorded in the author's previous work, *The Canadian Collector*.    One of these is the special Montreal section of the *Province of Ontario Gazetteer* for 1869 (Toronto, Robertson & Cook), which lists on page 626 the "St. Lawrence Glass Co., A. McK. Cochrane, Secty." Another is the *Dominion Directory* of 1871, which lists the "St. Lawrence Glass Works, Enoch Egginston, Supt.," with works situated in "Coteau

St. Augustin." Here we learn the name of the mysterious "experienced superintendent" mentioned but not named in the *Products and Manufactures*. The same *Directory* informs us that this was a sizable undertaking and employed the following workmen, all of whom lived in Coteau St. Augustin: William H. Grace, moulder; James H. Moore, finisher; Richard Davis, blower; J. H. Coley, blower; Patrick Herbert, blower; Thomas Jones, blower; George McCanal, blower; John Perkes, blower; and Robert Squire, blower.

The articles produced by this glass house appear to have included coal oil lamps ("various styles and sizes"), lamp chimneys ("of extra quality"), lamp shades ("Plain, Ground, and Cut Glass"), gas shades ("Plain, Ground and Cut Glass"). Tablewares consisted of "Goblets, tumblers, sugar-bowls, cream-jugs, spoon-holders, salt-cellars, castor-bottles, preserve dishes, nappies and water pitchers." There were also hyacinthe glasses, steam gauge tubes, glass rods, reflectors "or any other article made to order in White or Coloured Glass." In addition to these products the St. Lawrence Glass Company stocked kerosene burners, collars and sockets. It also advertised that "Druggist's Flint Glassware & Philosophical Instruments" were "made to order."

## 12. THE NORTH AMERICAN GLASS COMPANY GROUP (1879 — )

THIS CANADIAN glass house is the best known, the best documented and, to this writer, the most mysterious of all establishments in which glass has been manufactured. Its history began in St. Johns, P.Q., and will end at some far distant date.

In the beginning the story appears quite simple; the St. Johns works closes and moves to Montreal. So far so good; but twenty years later complications arise and fate decrees that even street names will change. The present company appears reluctant to co-operate with those who are interested in its beginnings. It may wish to compile a history of its own evolution. We hope that such a history will appear, for it would provide splendid source material to anyone interested in early twentieth century Canadian glass. The story of this house shows how hard a nineteenth century glass factory in Canada had to struggle in order to survive the fierce competition of glasswares imported from England, France, Belgium and the United States.

The story begins when the Foster Brothers relinquished their control of the glass works established in St. Johns in the 1850's (see chapter 10) and the Yuile Brothers took over. According to Mr. Joseph Jones, the Yuile Brothers "had purchased some land in Montreal at the corner of Mignonne and Parthenais Streets, and had decided to move the plant there."* His valuable letter continues with the information that the move was "done in 1880 with all the material that would be of any use."

Before continuing with Mr. Jones's letter it would be well to note that in 1879 the Yuile Brothers had established an "Office & wareroom— 479 St. Paul st. Montreal." This information, as well as any further data taken from Montreal directories, was provided in a letter dated March 21, 1959, from Mrs. Nellie Reiss, reference librarian of the Redpath Library at McGill University.

Mrs. Reiss must be commended for the time and effort s e has expended in research on Canadian glass, and for supplying a m ans of cross-checking several of the statements made by Mr. Jones. We may add that statements made by Mr. Jones as to locations, etc., which could be checked have proven to be correct in every detail.

Mr. Jones's letter continues:

The new building was on Parthenais Street, which consisted of a flint furnace which was upstairs as we called it, and a green tank on the ground floor. The flint furnace was a 12-pot square furnace, and the output was mostly chimneys and some press work, and a couple of prescription bottle shops. These shops were then connected with the A.F.W.U., but later on that department became amalgamated with what is known as the G.B.B.A.† On the Green Tank the output was mostly bottles, and under the management of Mr. Borland and the office clerk, Mr. Sawyer.

---

*This statement may be cross-checked in directories in the Reference Library, McGill University, Montreal.
†The Glass Bottle Blowers' Association of the United States and Canada, an official badge of which is in the Edith Chown Pierce and Gerald Stevens Collection in the Royal Ontario Museum.

Mr. Herdt, who had come to Montreal from France with his family, had become manager of the flint department, with his son, Henry Herdt, as office clerk.   As time went on Mr. Borland retired on account of poor health, and Mr. Herdt took charge of both flint and green.   The Flint Department was made up of workers from the States, and the Green by some of those who worked at St. Johns, and others from the States.

I forgot to mention the two brothers who worked at St. Johns, and one of them was Cook Crist and his brother Eugene. [For Eugene, see chapter 3.]   I feel sure that Cook went to work at Wallaceburg when it was known as the Sydenham Glass Company. . . .   In the meantime there was a pot furnace put in operation on Mignonne Street (five pots). A fire broke out I believe in 1885 which destroyed most everything some time in May of that year; only the pot furnace was left standing.   I am not sure, but I think it only ran for a couple of years.   During the vacation season the Company built a tank in its place which ran remarkably well, and the men made good wages.

As time went on the Company decided on extension, and the land adjoining was purchased, extending to Delormier Street, and a new plant was erected with three tanks under one roof and a flint furnace adjoining and equipped with more modern machinery at that time, and lehrs instead of ovens.   I am not too sure who then was manager of the new plant, but I feel pretty sure it was Donald Lamont.   He was followed by a man named Charles.   I cannot think of his last name; and then Dave Pugh.   I think you should know the rest (this to Mr. Davies of Wallaceburg), who in line took charge up to Mr. Bassett when the plant was moved to Wallaceburg. . . .

I forgot to mention that one year when the old plant was in operation the Company, the Yuile Brothers, brought some workers to Montreal from England and Jimmy Sephton's father was one of them.   Jimmy came to work in the new plant and snapped up for me and his father.   Later on he ran the finishing machine for us; . . . he went to the Machine Shop as an apprentice, and finally became head machinist and now, as you know, he is in charge at Hamilton (April, 1944).

The different names of the Company have been as follows: At St. Johns it was known as The Excelsior Glass Company.   When it moved to Montreal it was changed to The North American; then the Diamond; then Dominion. . . .

It has just occurred to me that at the plant at Parthenais Street the machinist and engineer was a man by the name of James Shaw, and I believe Tommy Hooag worked there.

Don't know if this will be of any interest to you or not, but at one time on the corner of Lagauchetière Street and Maisonneuve Street was a Garth Iron Works, and in the rear there was built a small dinky tank by a man named Dick Davis. . . .   It was for the purpose of making Beer Bottles of black glass. He got some workers from the North of England, but it did not last long and was closed down. The men returned to the Old Country.

The above, added to similar information supplied by Mr. George Gardiner of Hamilton gives ground for doubting that a complete record of persons attempting the manufacture of glass in Canada will ever be made. An unknown number of individuals made glass in "small dinky tanks" located on side streets in cities or rural communities. Thus we hear of "glass factories" which, though they can never be proven to have gone into production, tend to confuse the serious researcher.

Although Mr. Jones's letter is of great value, the information it supplies is most difficult to document. To attempt this we must begin with directories published in Montreal from 1879 to 1910, and one listing (there may be many but this is the only one known to this writer) contained in *The Home and Foreign Trade of Canada and Annual Report of the Commerce of Montreal*, 1880-1882 by Wm. J. Patterson, printed by D. Bentley & Co., 364 Notre Dame Street, Montreal in 1883.

This publication gives the following statistics: "Table XII.— Continued. Glass Works: Capital Invested, $307,000. Number of Hands Employed, 642. Total Annual Value of Products: $569,000." This was for the year 1881. Further on we find: "Glass Works: Number of Establishments—3. (These would have been the North American of Montreal and the Hamilton and Burlington works of Hamilton, Ontario.) Persons Employed: Male, 289, Female, 20. Amount of Works per annum, $108,200. Value of Raw Materials used. $83,400. Value of Articles produced, $230,000." On page 153 appears the following note: "The manufacture of Green and Flint Glass bottles for Druggists, and of Lamps, Lamp Chimneys, and other wares, is carried on extensively in Montreal. There is only one Factory at present, but it is of large capacity, and there is a ready market for all it turns out." The "one factory" was of course the Excelsior Glass Company, located at Mignonne and Parthenais Streets.

The development of this glass house can be followed from Montreal directories by noting the names by which it was successively known and the street addresses.*   In 1879 the Excelsior Glass Company was still at St. Johns, but it had an office and wareroom at 479 St. Paul Street, Montreal. In 1880 it moved to Montreal and located at Mignonne and Parthenais Streets.   From 1880 to 1884-1885 the name and location remained the same.   It appears that in 1885-1886 the firm changed its name to North American Glass Company.   From that year name and location remained unchanged until 1891 when the firm appears to have adopted the name Diamond Glass Company.

Under the new name, the firm's address remained the same until 1895, when the name of the street formerly known of as Mignonne was changed to De Montigny.   This has caused some confusion to researchers, since directories published in Toronto (the *Might 5 Cities Business Directory* for 1895) and Montreal for the same year appear to disagree. The name Diamond Glass Company continued until 1901-1902.   In that year the name was apparently changed to the Diamond Flint Glass Company, and the site changed to 179 Delormier Avenue.   In the amalgamation of 1913 the Diamond Flint Glass Co. Ltd. was merged with the Dominion Glass Co. Ltd. under the latter name.

A cross-check of the foregoing data is provided in the following excerpt from a letter received from Mrs. Nellie Reiss:

As for the Diamond Glass Company, by working backwards and forwards from the year 1897, it seems evident that this company existed for almost thirty years or longer under one name or other.   It began as the Excelsior Glass Company with an office and wareroom at 479 St. Paul in 1880-1881.   The next year it appears at Mignonne and Parthenais Streets, where it remained under that name until 1885-1886.   It then became the North American Glass Company.   In 1894-1895 Mignonne Street changed its name to De Montigny Street.   The Diamond Glass Company has a continuous listing from 1892-1893 to 1903-1904 when it became the Diamond Flint Glass Company, and so continued until 1910.   In this period there is also an entry for the North American Diamond Glass Company (Diamond Glass) from 1897-1898 to 1900-1901, but this has the same address as the Diamond Glass Company, i.e. 501 De Montigny.   In 1901-1902 the address for the Diamond Glass Company changed to 179 Delorimier Ave. and so continued until 1910.

---

*Apparent discrepancies in dates based on directories can be explained by the fact that directories normally reported information applicable to the year preceding the first named in the title.

The preceding data are of course obtained from directories only, not from persons or biased interests.

The commercial products of this glass house during its various phases are listed in advertisements. The almost unlimited production resulting from the amalgamation culminating in the Dominion Glass Co. Ltd., is such that historians of a later age may find that we have ignored much of importance. This work is concerned, however, only with special items that can be authenticated as having been produced in a Canadian glass house dating 1880-1913.

### SPECIMENS FROM THE EXCELSIOR GLASS COMPANY PERIOD

Information received from several sources visualize the extent and variety of whimseys produced by individual glass blowers working for this firm from the closing decade at St. Johns to the amalgamation of 1913. We know that the early Foster Brothers glass works specialized in special items made to commemorate a birthday, a marriage or other event, and that they could cut and engrave presentation pieces with the names or initials of individuals. We know, too, that this firm had presses specially made to produce goblets. The Yuile Brothers, founders of the North American Glass Company, may well have designed and produced the specialty known as the *Beaver goblet*, either before the move to Montreal or immediately afterward.

The *Beaver goblet* is a well-known and eagerly sought after piece, usually found today in the Province of Quebec, particularly in the Quebec City area. The reason for its popularity is quite evident. The upper half of the bowl bears a circle of six beavers, and the bottom shows three well designed maple leaves. Most important of all, around the outer edge of the foot or base is the embossed legend "St. Jean Baptiste. Quebec. 24 Juin 1880." This interesting collector's item measures $5\frac{1}{2}''$ in height. The bowl, which is oval, measures $3\frac{1}{4}''$ with the greatest circumference being 9". The circular base is $2\frac{3}{4}''$ in diameter. This piece is attributed to, but there is little doubt as to its origin.

The *Beaver goblet* is listed in S. T. Millard's book *Goblets II* where it is catalogued under "Unlisted and Unnamed" and then named *Beaver Band*." We have called it *Beaver*, but it could equally well be known as *Maple Leaf* or, possibly best of all, *St. Jean Baptiste*.

Another interesting item made at St. Johns during the Yuile Brothers régime (Excelsior Glass Company) is a typical St. Johns *goblet* of the plainest type. This commemorates the first Ottawa Exhibition, held in 1878. It is 5⅞″ in height, and is engraved with the legend "Exhibition 1878. A.R.D." According to the source from which this goblet was obtained, the initials indicate that the piece was purchased at the exhibition and engraved on the spot for a Mr. Denison. Without the engraving this rare item would have little interest to collectors.

Both goblets were made from a clear flint glass: the Beaver in a three-piece mould; the Exhibition in the usual two-piece type of mould so often used in Canadian glass works.

### SPECIMENS FROM THE DIAMOND FLINT GLASS COMPANY PERIOD

Thanks to several informants, the most important of whom is Mr. T. W. Bassett of the Dominion Glass Company Limited, the following special items have been authenticated as having been made in the Diamond Flint Glass Co.'s works in Montreal. In a letter received January 9, 1959, Mr. Bassett writes:

The glass paperweight containing my name (T. W. Bassett) which you saw here (Office of the President and General Manager, Beaver Hall Hill, Montreal) was made in the Delormier Avenue factory of the company in the year 1912. The plant was then owned by the Diamond Flint Glass Company Limited, which later became part of the Dominion Glass.

The reason for our having written Mr. Bassett stemmed from what may be called collector's luck. When we had called to interview Mr. Bassett, he was out of town. We were shown into his office, and there on a table was a *paperweight* similar in every respect but one (the name) to two weights in our collection. We had obtained both of these weights because we felt that they were of Canadian manufacture, and now it appeared that we had been correct in this conjecture. We examined the Bassett weight and were told that it had been made in Montreal—hence the letter to Mr. Bassett, and his reply.

These weights are quite distinctive, and are obviously made by the same glass blower or his apprentice. The Bassett weight is fashioned in the true glass paperweight shape, a circular dome-shaped body. All three are free-blown and cased in clear glass.

No. 34.   Free-blown Paperweights.   Diamond Flint Glass Company.   (*Circa* 1910).

The *T. W. Bassett paperweight* has an interior decoration resting upon a chipped-glass ground of assorted colours.   Above this floats a dove (?) with wings outspread and carrying a letter (?) in its beak.   Parallel to but under the dove is the name, then a stem, leaves and flowers resembling daisies.   The dove, name and flowers are in white.   We have not had the opportunity to measure this weight, but it is of the usual size.

The two additional weights, shown in Plate 34 are authenticated by their general features and by the use of the daisies.

No. 1 was made for a Mr. R. Dentist.   It measures 2⅛″ in height and 9½″ in circumference.   The ground consists of chips of glass coloured white, yellow and pink, not too finely ground after chipping.

No. 2 is slightly different from the two preceding pieces.   It bears the legend "I.O.O.F.," three links, a daisy and the letters "F.L.&T."   There are two daisy-like sprays on either side of the links. While it carries the name of a well-known fraternal society, the question arises: Could it have been made for the personal use of the glass blower? The ground differs in design, if not technique, from the others.   It is composed of chips coloured red, white and blue, with two shades of red being used.   These chips were worked into seven semi-funnel-like shapes rounding to and meeting at the centre.   Although this ground appears almost obtuse, it is a nice bit of craftsmanship.

These two glass paperweights date somewhere between 1902 and 1912.

### SPECIMENS FROM THE DOMINION GLASS COMPANY PERIOD

Although it is most difficult to obtain data relative to pieces other than those mass produced by the Montreal branch or branches of the present Dominion Glass (not to be confused with the Dominion Glass of the nineteenth century), it is known that individual glass blowers did on occasion demonstrate their wide knowledge of the medium. We have heard reports of pipes, drapes and similar items, including cuspidors but we have not as yet obtained authentic examples.

One type of commercial manufacture that deserves mention, however, is tableware made from beer bottles. We are informed that the Dominion Glass Company acquired large numbers of typical dark amber Canadian beer bottles and, breaking these up into a form of cullet, produced from them plates and other items of tableware. Although these were a commercial venture, they may in time be sought by collectors. It is always possible that the commercial product of today will become the collector's item of the future, if it is well made, unique, or otherwise historically interesting. *Beer-bottle plates* may be considered unique, and they are certainly interesting.

### 13. THE DOMINION GLASS COMPANY, MONTREAL (1886-1898)

THE EXISTENCE of this Canadian glass house was first brought to our attention through an article inspired by our book *In A Canadian Attic* in *Liberty* magazine. As a result of this, we received many letters telling of family pieces in the possession of persons living as far apart as Nova Scotia and British Columbia. Some of these letters were merely friendly, but others contained valuable data. One in particular mentioned the above company. Mrs. Gladys (Stewart) Mason of St. Lambert, P.Q., wrote to say that she had a glass *paperweight* made in the Dominion

Glass Works of Montreal in 1897. We had always considered any mention of a glass works bearing the name Dominion to refer to the existing company, but the date 1897 looked interesting. On our next visit to Montreal we called on Mrs. Mason and inspected the paperweight. One look told us that it was Canadian and had been made by Patrick (Pat) Wickham, who was known to have worked in Montreal *circa* 1897. We acquired the weight, returned home, studied our directories and discovered that the *Might 5 Cities Directory* for 1895 listed a Dominion Glass Co. Ltd. We then began our search for data relative to this company.

Directories are useful sources of information, and when you have the aid of such interested persons as Mrs. Nellie Reiss, reference librarian at McGill University you can learn much from them. Our own library includes several Montreal directories, but the McGill library has probably the most complete collection of directories in Canada especially of those relating to Montreal. Mrs. Reiss consulted these and dug up the following information: She wrote:

The Dominion Glass Company was the simplest one to trace. It first appeared in 1887-1888, located at Lafontaine and Papineau Streets. It last appeared at this location in 1899-1900. In the 1900-1901 directory a Dominion Glass Company is listed in the alphabetical section at De Montigny and Parthenais, but in the street section of the directory that is the location of the Diamond Glass Company. This might mean an error in the directory, or indicate an affiliation of the two companies. A Dominion Glass Company is not listed (again) before 1910, which is the last date checked.

As far as can be ascertained, the Diamond Flint Glass Company acquired the original Dominion Glass Company in 1898, as it was soon to acquire and amalgamate all glass manufacturing establishments. Up to that time the glass houses of Quebec, Ontario and the Maritimes had led a hand-to-mouth existence. With the introduction of better business management and technical know-how, the Canadian glass industry was enabled to meet the competition of glass imported from England, Belgium, France and the United States. Thus did the first firm in Canada to be known as the Dominion Glass Company lose its identity.

No. 35.    Free-blown Paperweight by Patrick (Pat) Wickham.    Dominion Glass Company (nineteenth century), Montreal, P.Q.    This weight is from a deep bluish aquamarine bottle glass.    Produced May, 1897.    Beer Bottle Plate.    Twentieth Century.
Dominion Glass Co. Ltd. (*Circa* 1940).

Thanks to the information supplied by Mrs. Mason, the documentation of directories, and the testimony of Mr. Gardiner that Patrick Wickham had worked in Montreal, we can authenticate one special piece produced by this nineteenth century Dominion Glass Company.

This as yet unique item is a typical *Wickham blown-glass weight* of a kind also found in Hamilton and Toronto.    It measures 1⅞″ in height and 10¼″ in circumference.    The body is of a glass coloured a very deep bluish-aquamarine.    In this floats the usual rectangular piece of opal glass upon which is written in lead pencil the legend "Alice—May 1897."

It is quite likely that in time we shall have a more detailed record of this Canadian glass house.    This strange reversal of the usual situation —knowledge of a special item without any data relating to the commercial products—is a revealing indication of how much remains to be done before we can have a complete history of glass-making in Canada.

# 3 The Glass Houses of Nova Scotia

# 3 The Glass Houses of Nova Scotia

14. THE NOVA SCOTIA GLASS COMPANY, TRENTON (1881-1892)

ONE OF THE most interesting and instructive references to nineteenth century Canadian glass is that which begins on page 176 of a work
entitled *Sketches of the Late Depression*, by Wm. Wickliffe Johnson,
(Montreal, J. T. Robinson, 1882). In a chapter headed "Crockery
Interest" we find the following:

Among other staple articles in this trade are coal oil lamps, lamp
chimneys, burners and wicks, fruit jars, goblets, and glass table ware,
all of which are now made largely here [in Canada]. Lamps are made
at Montreal and at New Glasgow, N.S. But as yet only the cheap lines
have been attempted [?], the more expensive goods being still imported.
Of chimneys, a very small proportion is now imported from Germany
or the United States, the glass factories at Montreal, Hamilton and
New Glasgow now turning out large quantities of an excellent quality.
A fair proportion of burners is now made here . . . the same remark applies
to wicks. . . . Up to this year, goblets, tumblers, and glassware generally
were not manufactured in Canada at all [?] . . . but the managers of the
glass factory recently established at New Glasgow, N.S., are showing
considerable activity and enterprise in this direction, and are now taking
orders for this class of goods from the wholesale trade, and their samples
are spoken of as being of good design and finish.

It will therefore be seen, as stated in the opening of this chapter,
that the conditions under which the trade is done have been largely
altered within the last few years, and for a good many lines we are not
dependent to so great an extent upon foreign markets as we formerly
were. This is especially true . . . of crockery and glassware.

137

This mention of Canadian glass, although it lightly brushes off the glass production of Ontario, is valuable to the student. It suggests that at that date (1881) the Vaudreuil factories had closed and it lists the proposed types later made in the earliest of Nova Scotian glass houses.

The late Edith Chown Pierce was convinced that glass was made in the Maritimes, though she had no proof of it, and equally certain that William Godkin Beach, manager of the Burlington Works, somehow identified with the Maritime glass industry during a decade she was otherwise unable to account for in her biography of him. Hoping to complete the work she had begun, her husband began independent investigations that ultimately led to a representative collection of early Nova Scotia glass in the Royal Ontario Museum. His findings were briefly reported in *Early Glass Houses of Nova Scotia* (The Ryerson Press, Toronto, 1958).

The greater part of the data contained in this section was obtained from three sources: Lorne Pierce's brochure; *Canadian Glass: A Footnote to History* by the late Edith Chown Pierce (privately printed, Toronto, The Ryerson Press, 1954); and the Nova Scotia Museum *Newsletter* (vol. 2, no. 3, April 1958), by George MacLaren. In addition to these three sources, we must include Mr. John W. Fraser, to whom Dr. Pierce's brochure is dedicated. Mr. Fraser, a "carrying-in" boy for the Nova Scotia Glass Company, aided greatly in the acquisition of authenticated pieces and data relative to all three glass houses operating in the Trenton-New Glasgow area.

The story begins in 1881 with a prospectus published in the *Eastern Chronicle*, a New Glasgow newspaper, which reads in part: "It is proposed to establish a glass company at Trenton for the manufacture of glassware such as tumblers, goblets and all kinds of glassware for general use. . . . Provisional Directors are Andrew Walker, James Eastwood, Graham Fraser, P. A. McGregor and A. C. Bell, M.P.P." Typically, the prospectus makes no mention of glass manufacturing in other areas. The company got under way in 1881.

It appears that the first manager was Mr. William Godkin Beach. If that was so, this new glass house was managed by a man who was one of the outstanding glass men of his time. Mr. Beach was born in Athens,

Leeds County, Ontario, in 1839.*  Of English stock, he was descended from a family who moved to Canada in the Loyalist migration.  He married Emily Dyde and they had one child, Elizabeth, born in 1864. The first proof we have that Mr. Beach was associated with glass-making in Canada is contained in a Hamilton *Directory* for the year 1878-1879, where he is listed with Murray A. Kerr.  The following year we find Beach listed as manager of the Burlington works, and he continues in this capacity until the *Directory* of 1882-1883 (information obtained in 1881), when he apparently moved to Nova Scotia.  Mr. Beach died in 1902, and was buried in Mount Pleasant Cemetery, Toronto.†

The first building of the Nova Scotia Glass Company was erected in 1881, and was situated one mile below New Glasgow and adjacent to the Intercolonial Railway.  Representatives of the company were sent to Europe and the United States, and glass blowers from Belgium, Bohemia and the United States were secured.  It is said that the foreign glass blowers were adaptable, and that "these fine people quickly fitted into the ways of the English and Scottish residents of the town."

We learned from Mr. William H. Harris, formerly sheriff of Pictou County, N.S., that the Registry of Deeds and Prothonotary's Office contains the following information, which we give in Mr. Harris's words:

The Nova Scotia Glass Company appears to have purchased land in Trenton in 1881, and was composed of New Glasgow business men. They sent Harvey Graham to Prague in March, 1883, to hire and bring out Bohemian glass blowers of whom one, Anton Jeykal, came out . . . to be a foreman . . . .  In 1889 Adam C. Bell was President, and Thomas Green and Andrew Walker were secretaries at different times.  Under date of June 9th, 1890, the Nova Scotia Glass Company sold their property for $2,000 to the Diamond Glass Company.  (The Nova Scotia works had a working capital at one time of approximately $100,000.)

The *Pictou News*‡ of June 3, 1883, carried this advertisement:

THE GLASS WORKS—The Nova Scotia Glass Works are now in full blast and are turning out a large amount of glass ware.  The number of hands at present on the pay roll is 160.  The wages paid weekly amount to over $1,000.

*First named Wiltsetown, then Farmersville, and later Athens, this village was the birth-place of the late Frank Stevens, Montreal Art Dealer and the father of the author.
†See *Canadian Glass: A Footnote to History.*
‡We quote freely from the brochures by George MacLaren and Lorne Pierce.

If the figures were as quoted, the cause of the failure is quite evident: an average wage of less than ten dollars a week, when glass blowers in Hamilton and other parts of the Dominion were "among the aristocracy of labour" and paid accordingly.

The reason for the choice of site on which this glass house was built appears to have been: "Because it possesses advantages for any amount of heavy manufacturing . . . cheap fuel (coal was close by), a supply of suitable sand (this was not used) and good shipping facilities. There is . . . within two or three miles of the town an extensive deposit of silica sand adapted for glass-making, and from which glass had actually been made (by whom, and at what date?)."

This interesting note continues with the statement: "It (silica sand) was found by a practical potter and glass-maker who came here from England . . . who afterwards went to Trenton, New Jersey. . . ."

The above data should be investigated because if true the "practical potter and glass maker" left New Glasgow fourteen or fifteen years before the establishment of the first proven Nova Scotia glass house. In other words, this unknown man was the first glass-maker in the Maritimes.

Other developments relative to this house are to be found in issues of the *Eastern Chronicle*. The *Halifax Morning Chronicle* of January 31, 1885, also gives an account of this glass house. The manager reported that the sales made during the previous year (1884) were between $90,000 and $100,000, but did not say whether this was a certified statement. The house employed "130 men and boys." (There were no laws forbidding child labour in Canada at that time.) The principal shipments were to Quebec (City?), Montreal and Toronto.

The following quotation suggests that this house decorated its pieces with both engraving and cutting (the engraving has been proven):

Fancy designs in pressed ware were made by holding the objects against revolving stones, using sand and oil. The stone called "Cragleith" was from a quarry of that name in Scotland. The cutters in the factory were mostly Bohemians. At least two types of sand were used [for cutting?]: fine white sand from Boston and brown coarser sand from Belgium. Articles made included lamp chimneys, lantern globes, chimneys for electric burner lamps, locomotive head-light chimneys (for the Grand Trunk, and Intercolonial Railway), tumblers of *twenty-one* different styles, and pepper and vinegar cruets.

According to Mr. John W. Fraser one room was used to store the moulds. When an order came for "five hundred or a thousand pitchers," the mould could only be released by the experts in charge. Even then the pitcher, when pressed, had to be inspected by the superintendent. Moulds were used for bottles and lantern globes; two- or three-section moulds being the most common. There was some attempt by the Belgians and Bohemians to introduce wooden moulds such as were sometimes used at Hamilton, but cast iron was the usual material from which the Nova Scotia moulds were made.

It appears that few if any commercial pieces were free-blown, and that the usual product was either pressed, or blown in a mould and finished by means of a snap.

### COMMERCIAL PRODUCTS SUGGESTED BY DOCUMENTATION

Goblets (twenty-one varieties)
Tumblers
Other tablewares
Lamp chimneys
Head-light chimneys (R.R.)
Vinegar cruets
Pitchers
Sugar bowls
Spoon holders
Lantern globes
Pepper (and salt?) shakers
Bottles

### COMMERCIAL PRODUCTS AUTHENTICATED BY MR. JOHN W. FRASER

Cheese dish and cover
Water pitcher
Cream pitcher
Egg cup
Glass hat (tumbler)
Preserve dish
Sugar bowl
"Victoria" cake plate

### WHIMSEY TYPES PRODUCED BY ALL NOVA SCOTIAN GLASS HOUSES

Glass canes (these in some numbers)
Glass drapes (William Godkin Beach brought glass blowers from Hamilton)
Glass chains (merely chains—not drapes)
Free blown hats
Hammers (various types—some should be found in and about Trenton)
Pipes (these were made in all Canadian glass houses)
Swords (both swords and pipes could be attributed to Hamilton workers)

No. 36.   Glendinning Cheese Dish.   Diamond Glass Company.

### AUTHENTICATED SPECIMENS

The following pieces were acquired by Dr. Lorne Pierce, and are now in The Edith Chown Pierce and Gerald Stevens Collection of Canadian Glass in the Royal Ontario Museum:

A *cheese dish* donated by Mr. Charles A. Glendinning, C.A., of New Glasgow. This dish with bell-shaped cover, 8″ x 8″, was made for the first wife of John K. Stewart of New Glasgow "over seventy years ago." Mr. Glendinning's father worked in the sorting room of the Diamond Glass Co. when John W. Fraser was employed there. The name "Mrs. J. K. Stewart" is engraved on the cover. The finial on the cover is of the baluster type, and the bell-shaped body of the cover has a slight design consisting of two narrow bands of a ribbed pattern. The base is approxi-

No. 37.  Water Pitcher and MacKinnon Cream Pitcher.  Diamond Glass Company.

mately 11″ in diameter and has a pressed pattern resembling that known as "waffle."  The narrow flared rim is ribbed in a manner similar to that on the cover or dome.  This piece was made from a clear flint non-lead glass.

A *water pitcher* authenticated by Mr. Fraser, who stated: "I can remember when I used to carry the same type of pitchers to the tempering lehr."  This flint glass pitcher has a pressed design consisting of grapes, leaves and vine, and a narrow band of ribbing.  The base, which is slightly flared, has a leaf design encircling it in full.  The handle is not applied, but is part of the three-piece mould.  This piece is 8¾″ in height and in proportion.

A *cream pitcher* donated to the Collection by Mrs. Eunice MacKinnon of New Glasgow.  This is a companion piece to the water pitcher, and is 5¼″ in height.

No. 38.   MacKinnon Queen Victoria Plate.   Diamond Glass Company.

A *glass hat*, an interesting specimen as yet unique for Canada.   A number are known to have been made in other countries, particularly the United States, but the usual Canadian specimens were either free-blown or of a commercial pressed-glass type sold as novelties.   This particular piece began as a moulded tumbler but the glass blower—possibly trained in the U.S.A.—reheated the lip or upper edge in the glory hole and, pressing the softened edges on the marver or something similar, flared the rim so that it resembled the brim of a hat.   Dr. Pierce states: "A tumbler, of fluted design, with a rolled lip on two sides, 3¼" high, donated by Mrs. Ella Steele Munn, Westville, N.S., a cousin of John W. Fraser."   This item was made from a clear flint glass.

In addition to these there are preserve dishes and sugar bowls, and, most important of all from the collector's viewpoint, a *Queen Victoria plate* (mentioned in the introduction).

No. 39. "Victoria" design used by many Canadian glass houses. This pattern is said to have been made 1885-1915.

The authentication of the latter acquired from Mrs. Eunice McKinnon of New Glasgow, was a splendid bit of research on the part of both Pierce and Fraser. The importance of this piece is that it opens many doors to the Canadian collector, doors that lead to rooms filled with several types of cake plates, cup plates, compotes and other tableware. Although this design was quite obviously either of English or Canadian origin, the majority of collectors credited it to the United States. Such Victoria pieces as are acquired in Canada—and do not have a lacy decoration added to the Victoria design—may well be credited, however, to the growing list of Canadian patterns. The best known Canadian pieces, found in great numbers between Nova Scotia and the Wallaceburg section of Ontario, consist of two somewhat different types. The first, that authenticated by Pierce, is shown in Plate 38. This measures 10″ x 11¾″, and is usually found in a flint glass*. The second is quite obviously from a similar source, and although it differs in many respects the basic design, especially that of the portrait, is the same. This is shown in Plate 39. One additional point in favour of the authentication of this second type is the inclusion of the St. Andrew's Cross of the flag of Nova Scotia, a cross forming part of the design used on tableware attributed to the Humphrey Glass Works of Trenton, N.S., and used extensively by Nova Scotians as a motif in various media. This piece too, measures 10 x 11¾″.

There are several designs and types "attributed to," and "said to have been made by," which are doubtful and do not deserve mention in this work. There are also glass canes in very great numbers which are attributed to this glass house. Glass canes as such are of little significance to the collector. It is not sufficient evidence to have someone state that "My grandfather said he bought it at the . . . glass works in the year . . ." Canada appears to be filled with glass canes, and every one authentic.

### 15. The Humphrey Glass Works: Trenton, N.S. (1890-1914);
### Moncton, N.B. (1915-1920)

ACCORDING TO Mr. George MacLaren, this glass house was first established in the "backyard" of John Humphrey. It appears that Mr. Humphrey "learned the trade of glass-making in Pittsburgh, Pennsylvania." If so, this Canadian (he appears to have gone to Pittsburgh from Trenton) was trained in what was to become one of the most important glass centres in the United States. With such a background John Humphrey was well qualified to introduce a third and competitive glass house to the area.

---

*A number of similar specimens have been seen made from a glass coloured a medium-deep amber.

Is it not strange that the Nova Scotian towns of Trenton and New Glasgow attracted so many persons interested in glass-making? Was it that glassmen could not resist the lure of the unused sand deposits, or was it that the Maritime Province seemed to have a potential much greater than that of Quebec, Ontario or the west, which formed the *raison dêtre* of the Humphrey Glass Works? Questions without an answer! But they applied to many a Canadian glass house established in the nineteenth century. At any rate, Humphrey's began with the manufacture of bottles, fruit jars, lamp chimneys and lantern globes. In addition to these basic items they produced "glass rolling-pins [since found in some numbers], fly traps (?), patent medicine bottles and flasks." Mr. MacLaren continues: "During 1907-1908 soda water bottles were a specialty," and "Special attention was given to private moulds." This mention of the ability of Humphrey workers to produce moulds made to order suggests that there were many specific types of pattern and decoration used by this house, and we are indebted to Dr. Pierce, Mr. Fraser and, in particular, Mr. MacLaren for the authentication of several specimens. In addition to these specimens there are several pieces attributed to this house which could very well be authentic. The most important in this last category is a design named for us by Mrs. J. D. Robinson of Toronto "Tassel and Crest."

It appears that this glass house was located on several successive sites, the first was the backyard of Mr. Humphrey's town lot. A fire occurring *circa* 1900 resulted in the choosing of a second location in 1901. Both Pierce and MacLaren state that the new plant was set up in 1901 at the end of Glass Street (Trenton). The third site was a new departure for the Nova Scotia glassmen—a move out of the province to Moncton, New Brunswick.

The following would be a reasonably accurate listing of sites and dates:

Humphrey's backyard (Trenton): 1899 or 1900

Glass Street (Trenton): 1901-1914

Moncton: 1915-1920 (the closing date)

No. 40. The Staff of Humphrey Glass Works, Trenton, N.S. (about 1907).  Top left: John (Jock) Humphrey; Left, second row: Eddie Humphrey; Immediately below (with white collar): W. D. McKay, bookkeeper; Man with arms folded: Wheeler; Seated left, bottom row: Edgar Humphrey; Second from left: Johns S. Fraser; Third from left: James Davidson: Standing extreme right: Benjamin Humphrey, Boy seated on bench, fourth in: Gussie Grant (still living); Front row right (immediately behind second boy): Ray Livingstone (owner of this picture, still living).

Although this glass house would at first appear to have been the most successful of the Maritime attempts at glass-making, this conjecture is proven incorrect by evidence obtained from reliable sources. In 1905 an Act was passed by the Nova Scotia Legislature to exempt the Humphrey Glass Company from taxation. It authorized the county of Pictou to make the exemption for a period not exceeding fifteen years, on the condition that the company continued glass-making efficiently. Even with almost ideal conditions under which to operate, the Humphrey works appears to have lost ground to the competition provided by the Dominion Glass Company, and at last, in 1920, it banked its fires for good.

In April, May and June, 1913, the company was advertising for boys.* Whether or not the demand was satisfied, the Humphrey works closed and moved out of the province. What could have necessitated such a move when the home town approved a tax-free existence if efficiency was maintained?

According to several sources, it appears that the move to Moncton was decided upon because of the accessibility of natural gas from which to obtain the heat necessary to melt a batch. In Moncton the Humphreys collected "considerable capital" from those interested in adding a new industry to the city. All went well until "after two years, the stockholders were not satisfied with the way things were going, and had some difficulty with the Humphreys, who withdrew from the business."

We do not know the names of the new officers or of the glass blowers. But it appears that they had little success. The new management is said to have withdrawn from the manufacture of glass because of an increase in the gas rate. Mr. MacLaren states:

In 1919 the gas rates to commercial users went up by 50%, which made it prohibitive for the melting of glass. Besides this, they were not able to go in for the manufacture of . . . glassware . . . because of the competition the Dominion Glass Company gave them. While here [in Moncton] the extent of the activity was lamp chimneys and globes.

*Boys, i.e. carrying-in boys, were not apprentices. The Canadian apprentice was a man who had worked in a glass house for a sufficient number of years to learn the basic techniques. When he had arrived at an age and a knowledge warranting further training he was apprenticed and after a period usually of four to five years he became a fully qualified glass blower, with the prestige and high rates of pay demanded by expert craftsmen.

Thanks to Dr. Bruce Fergusson and Mr. Donald C. MacKenzie, we have the names of some of the glassmen associated with this firm. Dr. Pierce states:

Dr. Bruce Fergusson sends the following list of the Humphrey family employed in the glass works. (The spelling varies between Humphrey and Humphreys in lists, advertisement and directories.)

> J. M. M. Humphreys, president
> Benjamin Humphreys, foreman
> Duncan Humphreys, employee
> Edgar T. Humphreys, director
> Edward C. Humphreys, director
> Ephraim H. Humphreys, general manager
> Forest Humphreys, glass worker

Mr. Donald C. MacKenzie, of the National Museum, Ottawa, presented the author with a copy of *McAlpine's Nova Scotia Directory*, 1907-1908.   Directories of this type are hard to come by and are much sought after by librarians and researchers.   Although this particular work belongs to the twentieth century, it lists many Maritime craftsmen working in the nineteenth and, in particular, both an advertisement paid for by the Humphrey Glass Co. of Trenton and a list of glass workers associated with this house.   The advertisement reads:

HUMPHREYS GLASS CO.
Limited.

manufacturers of all kinds of

BOTTLES, FRUIT JARS
Lamp Chimneys and Lantern Globes

SODA WATER BOTTLES
a specialty.

Special Attention Given to Private Moulds

T R E N T O N ,   N . S .

Phone 69J.                                                      P.O. Box 40.

The following persons were associated with this house in 1906:

George Clish, glass blower
E. H. Humphreys, sec.-treas.
John M. Humphreys, president
Walker Liddle, glass blower
Walker Little [?] glass blower

Lena Matheson, stenographer
Daniel McEachern, glass blower
Simon McLellan, glass blower
Charles Miller, glass blower
Rod Ross, glass worker

## ARTICLES AUTHENTICATED BY DOCUMENTATION

Bottles
Fruit jars
Medicine bottles

Lamp chimneys
Lantern globes
Flasks (commercial)

Rolling-pins
Fly traps
Soda water bottles

## PRODUCTS AND WHIMSEYS AUTHENTICATED OR ATTRIBUTED TO

Bottles
Egg cups
Hammers (glass)
Goblets (plain)
Cream pitchers

Chimneys
Free-blown hats
Cornucopia (glass horns)
Canes (glass)
Spoon holders

Covered dishes
Witch balls
Chains (glass)
Preserve dishes
Covered sugar bowls

## SPECIFIC ITEMS PRODUCED BY OR ATTRIBUTED TO THIS GLASS HOUSE

The following pieces were acquired by Dr. Lorne Pierce and Mr. John W. Fraser:

A flint glass, very plain *goblet* donated to The Edith Chown Pierce and Gerald Stevens Collection in the Royal Ontario Museum by Mrs. Daniel Daley, East River Road, New Glasgow. It measures 6″ in height and is typical of the clear class undecorated goblet manufactured by Canadian glass houses in very great numbers, a type which is difficult to authenticate unless obtained from a local source.

A *glass chain* was donated to the Edith Chown Pierce and Gerald Stevens Collection by Mrs. William Hughes, East River Road, New Glasgow. This authentic specimen of a flint glass non-lead chain was presented by Mrs. Hughes as a souvenir of the old days of the Humphrey works in which her brother, the maker of the chain, blew glass. Although these Nova Scotian chains do not exhibit the mastery shown in chains and drapes originating in Ontario, they indicate that, given the colours and types of glass known to have been used in Upper Canada, the glass blowers of the Maritimes could have produced for posterity examples of whimsey know-how that would have equalled those of Quebec and Ontario. In other words, any qualified Canadian glass blower, in whatever province, could have produced commercial or off-hand objects second to none.

A *glass cane* is described by Pierce as follows: "This blown glass cane, 38″ long, with crook, was purchased from ex-Sheriff William H. Harris, 80 Water Street, Pictou, N.S. It was given to his father by one of the glass workers of Trenton."

A *comport and cover* is listed as "attributed to," but attributions follow so thick and fast that the author feels that the term "authenticated" should be applied. Dr. Pierce attributed this design to the Humphrey glass house. So do Mr. Fraser and Mr. MacLaren. The author cannot find a similar design accredited to any glass house, nor does he himself know of anything similar, and his library includes many of the books on glass published in England and the United States. May we therefore credit the "Tassel and Crest" pattern to the Humphrey glass house of Trenton, Nova Scotia? If any reader knows of a similar design credited to a glass house in any country in Europe or America, he is asked to write to the author. The author feels that a great number of pressed glass designs, rightly designated by the general term "American Glass," originated in that section of North America which comprises the Dominion of Canada. This belief is based on the design named by Mrs. J. D. Robinson "Tassel and Crest." The author makes no claim to have studied every book published on glass, but none of those he has read mentions or shows this particular pattern.

This design is found in several patterns embodied in one or more pieces, the most complicated of which is that in the covered comport illustrated in Plate 41. Although the illustrations must be studied to evaluate the whole design, a description of the components may be helpful. The *cover* appears to have been made in a two-piece mould. The finial consists of a triple plume, somewhat similar to the crest of the Prince of Wales. The sloping shoulder has an all-over pattern quite like that named by Ruth Webb Lee "Herringbone"; in this instance the closeness of the pattern supplies almost an optical illusion. The flared side has a four-part design consisting of an upper ring of attached semi-circles, dots and pendants and an upsidedown crown or script W. Immediately under the stepped edge is a ring of semicircles forming *the base*, the points and arches of which

No. 41.   Comport and Cover.   The Humphrey Glass Works.

are supplied with elements similar to those on the side of the cover. The *main designs* comprise two elements, one of which in particular is thought to be unique. The most important is an element which at first glance resembles the Thunderbird totem of the West Coast Indians, but really consisting of crossed trumpets, a small shield upon which is a Saint Andrew's cross, four halved feathers, and other embellishments. The second element is that of a palm tree having five branches and two coconuts. The bottom of the bowl and the base are decorated with rayed ribbing.

These pieces, of which there are several, measure approximately 10″ in height overall, and the greatest width is about 7″. The three best known examples are that in the author's collection, that in The Edith Chown Pierce and Gerald Stevens Collection, and that in the Nova Scotia Museum at Halifax. All known specimens are of a good quality flint glass.

In addition to covered comports the following pieces are known to have been made in the Tassel and Crest design: preserve dishes, cream pitchers, spoon holders and covered sugar bowls.

## 16. The Lamont (Diamond) Glass Company, Trenton (1890-1902)

MR. WILLIAM H. HARRIS of Pictou supplied Dr. Pierce with the following information, gleaned from the Registry of Deeds and Prothonotary's Offices:

Under the name of the Lamont Glass Company, David Lamont and Donald Lamont formed a partnership June 30, 1891, and manufactured glassware.

The name of Donald Lamont is one of the most important in the history of Canadian glass. Although we do not know where he served his apprenticeship, or from whom he learned the practical and business aspects of glass-making, we do know that Mr. Lamont was one of the few Nova Scotians who continued in the glass industry after the closing of his glass works. In chapter 12 we found that Donald Lamont was at one time manager of the North American glass works. Indeed, it is interesting to compare the names of glassmen of the executive type interested in the old North American works of Montreal with those of the Lamont Glass Company of Trenton.

The best documentation so far obtained is that supplied by Dr. Bruce Fergusson, Archivist of Nova Scotia. According to Dr. Fergusson, the Lamont Glass Works ran in *McAlpine's Nova Scotia Directory*, from 1890-1897, an advertisement that read:

David Lamont                    Henry Lamont                    Donald Lamont

## LAMONT GLASS WORKS

—Manufacturers of—

A general Line of Blown and Cut Glassware

Green and Flint Bottles of all Kinds

Cut Door Lights a Specialty

Trenton, New Glasgow, N.S.

This firm encountered difficulties, and on April 1, 1898, leased its plant to the Diamond Glass Company, which ran the North American Glass Works of Montreal. Although the old St. Johns works, of St. Johns, P.Q., had long disappeared, the glassmen attracted to Canada by the house established by the Foster brothers were still dominating the Canadian scene. The Diamond Glass Company was acquiring systematically every non-prodcutive or non-paying glass establishment— glass houses which would otherwise have closed their doors and extin- guished their fires without making any provision for their trained employees. The Diamond Glass Company kept glass-making alive in Canada and added many well trained glassmen to its staff.

The lease being signed, the new management from Montreal took over, with William Yuile, president, and D. Williamson, secretary, both of Diamond Glass, now in control. It appears that the Lamonts remained in charge of the works until, on August 1, 1902, The Diamond Glass Company sold:

all their lands (including the property bought from the Nova Scotia Glass Company, and the property known as the Lamont Glass Factory) to Bailey-Underwood, a firm manufacturing farm machines, with the stipulation that is was not to be used as a glass works. The property sold for $1,150, and the deed is signed by D. Williamson, Secretary.*

Mr. J. W. Fraser† visited the Lamont works several times in his youth, and supplies the following important data:

This plant was situated almost on the boundaries of the towns of New Glasgow and Trenton and was a hive of industry in the early days. Donald Lamont was a genius in glass production, being without peer in either of the other two glass concerns. They produced quite a bit of coloured glass (?), turning out some very fine electric wares and lamp shades. Their expert glass mixer was William F. MacDonald, a New Glasgow man who is still alive in his eighty-seventh year (1958).

Mr. Donald Lamont's association with Canadian glass continued for over fifty years. After closing of the Lamont Glass Company he moved to Montreal, where he was employed by the Diamond Glass Company. In 1906 he resigned and moved to Vancouver, B.C., where a new glass house had been established. This house banked its fires in 1908. In 1911 Mr. Lamont was employed by the Manitoba Glass Co., of Winnipeg, with plant located at Beauséjour. In 1913 he was moved to the newly established Dominion Glass Company factory at Redcliff, Alberta, where he "was privileged to light the first two furnaces." From Redcliff he moved to Montreal, and from there—still with Dominion Glass—he went to Wallaceburg. In his lifetime Mr. Lamont played a part in extending the glass industry of Canada from coast to coast. He confirms the truth of the old glass-maker's saying, "Once a glassman, always a glassman."

*Early Glass Houses of Nova Scotia.
†Mr. Fraser retired from his work in the composing room of The Evening News, New Glasgow, N.S., in 1959, and died early in 1960.

No. 42. MacKenzie Spoon Holder, Lamont Glass Company. Munn Glass Hat, Diamond Glass Company. MacKenzie Tumbler, Lamont Glass Company.

### AUTHENTICATED SPECIMENS

Although it has so far been impossible to obtain examples of the Lamont coloured or cut glass, the following specimens in other categories have been acquired for The Edith Chown Pierce and Gerald Stevens Collection:

A unique *spoon holder*, a personalized although commercial item, is interesting not only in its being an authenticated Lamont product but more especially in its having been made for a specific person. The basic decorations consist of two narrow ribbed hands typical of all three Nova Scotian glass houses, and a gently scalloped rim. The uniqueness is the result of an engraved and cut decoration consisting of foliage and the initials "M.F." which stand for Mary Fraser. It is 4½" in height, and is shown in illustration No. 42.

A very thin glass *tumbler* 3½″ in height and 2½″ in width, is interesting because of a sand-blasted design consisting of the Lord's Prayer on one side. It was obtained from Mrs. George MacKenzie of New Glasgow and is now in the Edith Chown Pierce and Gerald Stevens Collection.

A *glass cane* rarely included in important collections. This specimen is a glass whimsey of a kind which merits mention on account of its undoubted authenticity. It is a blown piece 38″ in length, with crook. It was acquired from ex-Sheriff William H. Harris of Pictou, who stated that it was given to his father by one of the glass workers. Mr. Fraser related that one of the old glass blowers of the area recalled a Natal Day celebration held in Trenton. On that occasion "numerous floats and displays of products were witnessed by thousands of spectators. One thing most original in the parade was a body of glass employees, each carrying a glass cane." Mr. Gardiner of Hamilton stated to the author that a contingent of glass blowers walking in a Labour Day parade in Toronto included sections of men carrying glass revolvers, glass swords, glass hatchets and glass canes—the last being the easiest of all to make.

A *lamp chimney* was donated by Mr. William Fraser MacDonald of New Glasgow, a qualified glass blower who had worked for both the Lamont and Dominion companies, and who had made and witnessed the making of vast numbers of similar pieces. Although a purely commercial product, it is the best documented of all. It is a typical chimney of a late period, 9″ in height. It is finished off with a beaded rim not at all similar to the crimped rims produced in the Burlington branch of the Diamond Glass Company at Hamilton, Ontario.

# 4 *Canadian Stained and Cut Glass*

# 4 *Canadian Stained and Cut Glass*

## 17. ROBERT MCCAUSLAND LIMITED, TORONTO (1856— )

GLASS STAINING is a distinct art, not to be confused with glass manufacturing. The first step is the drawing of a small sketch of the proposed design; a design suitable for the purpose and involving research into background, subject matter, and conditions of lighting, both daylight and artificial. The painting (staining) of the glass itself is done by one of many available methods. Then comes the firing and glazing. The glass is removed from the easel and placed in the kiln, where the pigment is fused and becomes a part of the glass.

Although we know that the art of painting and staining glass was practised in Canada some years before, the Robert McCausland establishment appears to have been the first of its type in the Dominion. As the company is still in existence we can obtain data direct from the source, and we can check these data to some extent by means of directories.

The first indication of an establishment for staining glass in Upper Canada was obtained from the *Canada Directory*, 1857-1858. In this is found the entry, "McCausland & Bullock, glass stainers, Temperance near Bay St. (Toronto)." The present "Robert McCausland, 214 John Street." We do not know the year in which Mr. Bullock or his successors ceased to appear in the firm name, but a pamphlet issued by the present-day firm provided the following excerpts:

Artists in Stained Glass since 1856. (This statement is confirmed by the previously mentioned *Canada Directory*).
In 1870 . . . shipment made its way by rail, steamer and "Red River Cart" up to the then little-known Fort Garry, now Winnipeg (Manitoba),

for the church being erected by the late Rev. Dr. George Young. These windows are referred to at length in his interesting book, *Manitoba Memories*. To All Saints' Cathedral, Aklavik, on the fringe of the Arctic circle, went a series of subject windows.

The first Stained Glass to enter the Yukon Territory left here in 1901 . . . while the trails were still carrying their crowd of eager gold-seekers. From Hay River . . . came another order: many hundreds of miles this shipment travelled by dog-sled . . . and there it stands today.

According to the McCausland pamphlet, additional shipments went to Galveston, Texas; San Jose, Costa Rica; Cleveland and Chicago in the United States. Nearer home are a series of windows in Mount Carmel College, Niagara Falls, Ontario, and other examples in Grace Church, Brantford, and in the City Hall, and Timothy Eaton Memorial Church in Toronto.

In addition to stained glass windows this company may be credited with many lantern-type lighting fixtures made from metal-cased sheets of stained glass. This out-of-doors type of lantern was used to embellish nineteenth century driveway entrances.

The McCauslands stained, cut and decorated glass, but did not manufacture glass from raw material. Only establishments listed as glass houses or glass-makers performed this last operation.

## 18. Clapperton and Sons Limited, Toronto (1905 — )

THE FACT that glass cutting was done in Canada fifty years ago is attested by a very rare periodical *The Canadian Pottery and Glass Gazette*, published in Toronto by Publishers Limited. Its issue for April, 1908 (vol. 2, no. 2) contains the information that Gundy-Clapperton Co., 61 Albert Street, Toronto, made "nothing but cut glass, and nothing but the best."

No. 43. Late Victorian (1890-1910) pressed glass pattern produced in many Canadian glass houses (check in Eaton's Catalogue). Design could be listed as "Pointed Bull's Eye". Two Cut Glass Tumblers decorated with designs cut by the Gundy-Clapperton Company (now Clapperton & Sons Ltd.), Toronto, Ontario. (*Circa* 1909). The first (*left*) illustrates the cutting listed as "Classic"; the second (*right*) shows the design originated by this firm and known as the pattern "D", a design the simplified version of which is in use at the present time.

No. 44. Punch Set decorated with a cut "Grape Panel" design originated by Gundy-Clapperton (now Clapperton & Sons Ltd.) of Toronto, Ontario. (*Circa* 1909).

Gundy-Clapperton is now Clapperton & Sons, Ltd., 23 River Street, Toronto.   This company supplied the following information:

We did not at any time make glass but we do our own cutting and design our own patterns.   The blanks were obtained formerly from the following firms: the Baccarat Glass Company of France, the Val St. Lambert Glass Company of Belgium, the Libbey Glass Company of Toledo, Ohio (U.S.A.), the H. C. Fry Glass Company of Rochester, Pa. (U.S.A.), the Union Glass Company of Summerville, Mass. (U.S.A.) and the Dorflinger Glass Company, U.S.A.   The last three of these firms have been out of business for some time.   All our full crystal blanks are now imported from the Val St. Lambert Glass Company (Belgium).

It appears that this Canadian company was founded by Mr. G. H. Clapperton in 1905, and that the Gundy-Clapperton Company was formed in 1906.   Within a few years the original management took control, and the firm has since been known under its present title.

Glass cutting of a sort has been practised in Canada from the mid-nineteenth century.   The earlier efforts consisted of decorations on special items or orders.   In other words, nineteenth century Canadian cut glass was not true cut glass as we know it today.

From Mr. W. M. Clapperton we secured a catalogue, dated before World War 1, which contains illustrations of the types of cutting offered to the Canadian market of the time.   These include Hob Star, Colonial, Coronation, Nepture, Hob Flare, Wheat, Buzz, Metro, Norman, Keystone, Classic, Maple Leaf, Mayflower, Floral, Zesta, Antony, Duncan, Touchstone, Strawberry, Grape, Cordelia, Marguerite and many other designs.

The objects decorated with these designs included punch sets, bowls, fruit nappies, butter plates and tubs, colognes, wine sets, decanters and stemwares, jugs, and tumblers, water bottles and plateaux, lamps, candlesticks and candelabra, nut, cream and mayonnaise bowls and plates, oil and vinegar bottles, marmalades, olive trays, pickle trays, etc.   Indeed, this Canadian firm used all of the popular patterns and forms, and originated a number of its own.

No. 45.  A design used by Canadian glass houses.  The Maple Leaf,
Crest, and the word "Canada" are proof which substantiate the oral
claim of a Canadian origin.

No. 46. The Maple Leaf is of course Canadian. This motif is one which has supplied Canadian glass houses with an endless variation; a variation resulting in glass designs typical of this nation.

Mr. G. H. (Harry) Clapperton, then only a boy of twelve, moved in 1885 to Toledo, Ohio, from his birthplace in Stourbridge, England. In 1900 Mr. Clapperton, now a qualified glass cutter, came to Canada, and was employed by Gowans-Kent. It is thought that Clapperton was the originator of Gowans-Kent cut glass, and this theory is supported by an advertisement in the *Toronto Directory* for the year 1897 that reads "Gowans, Kent & Co. Wholesale Crockery and Glassware" and makes no mention of manufacturing.

In 1905 Mr. Clapperton went into business on his own, and in the following year he joined with Mr. N. F. Gundy to form the Gundy-Clapperton Company. In 1921 he formed the firm of Quinte-Clapperton Amalgamated and opened a plant in Deseronto. In 1931 fire destroyed the plant at Deseronto, and the Clapperton firm returned to its first home, Toronto.

The best known of the earlier patterns originating from the wheel of this Canadian artist in cut glass are Norman, Maple Leaf, Classic, Geisha, and many variations of floral designs.

We are informed that modern methods differ very little from those of fifty years ago, except that cuttings are not so elaborate. As in many other types of hand-made wares, however, changes in consumer taste and rising costs of production have led the manufacturer to adopt less complicated motifs—a circumstance which results in collectors' items less than fifty years old.

# 5 Twentieth Century Canadian Glass Houses

# 5 Twentieth Century Canadian Glass Houses

ALTHOUGH THE general subject of this work is nineteenth century Canadian glass, it is necessary to include several glass houses established after the turn of the century in order to provide some documentation of glass houses whose names may be encountered in newspapers, reports and directories.

The Cayuga glass house was first brought to our attention by Mr. H. Pearson Gundy, Librarian of Queen's University, Kingston, Ontario. Mr. Gundy was doing research on early imprints and, in the somewhat rare publication *Statutes of His Majesty's Province of Upper Canada Passed in the First Session of the Twelfth Provincial Parliament of Upper Canada by Authority Sir John Colborne, K.C.B., Lieutenant Governor* (Toronto, printed by Robert Stanton, Printer to the King's Most Excellent Majesty), encountered a statute entitled "An Act for Incorporating certain Persons therein named, and their Associates, under the Style and Title of the Cayuga Glass Manufacturing Company," and passed on April 16, 1835. It reads in part:

I. *Whereas* the establishment of Glass Works in this Province would greatly conduce to the advantage of the Inhabitants thereof; *And whereas* John De Cow, Samuel Wood, Jacob Upper, George Rowe, William Hepburne and others, by their Petition have prayed for the privilege of being Incorporated for the promotion of that object: *Be it therefore enacted* by the King's Most Excellent Majesty, by and with the advice and consent of the Legislative Council and Assembly of the Province of

Upper Canada, constituted and assembled by virtue of, and under the authority of an Act passed in the Parliament of Great Britain, entitled, "An Act to repeal certain parts of an Act passed in the fourteenth year of His Majesty's reign, entitled, 'An Act for making more effectual provision for the Government of the Province of Quebec, in North America, and to make further provision for the Government of the said Province'," and by the authority of the same, That the said John De Cow, Samuel Wood, Jacob Upper, George Rowe, William Hepburn, together with all such other persons as hereafter shall become Stockholders of the said Glass Works, shall be and are hereby ordained, constituted and declared to be a Body Corporate and Politic, in fact and by the name of the Cayuga Glass Manufacturing Company. . . .

II. *And be it further enacted by the authority aforesaid*, That a Share in the said Glass Manufacturing Company shall be Six Pounds Five Shillings, and the number of Shares shall not exceed One Thousand Six Hundred, and that the whole amount of the Stock, Estate and Property . . . shall never exceed in value Ten Thousand Pounds.

III. *And be it further enacted by the authority aforesaid*, That Books of Subscription shall be opened within one month after the passing of this Act, in the District of Niagara . . . at a Meeting to be held . . . for that purpose. . . .

IV. *And be it further enacted by the authority aforesaid*, That as soon as the sum of One Thousand Pounds shall have been subscribed, it shall and may be lawful . . . to call a Meeting . . . for the purpose of proceeding to the Election of the numbers of Directors. . . .

XIV. *And be it further enacted by the authority aforesaid*, That the Shares of the said Capital Stock shall be transferable, and may from time to time be transferred by the respective persons so subscribing the same: *Provided always*, that such transfer be entered or registered in a book or books to be kept for that purpose by the Directors.

XVI. *And be it* (etc.), That it shall and may be lawful for the Directors to commence the operations of the said Company as soon as Five per Cent shall be paid in on the Capital Stock subscribed as aforesaid.

XVII. *And be it* [etc.], That the said Company may construct the said Glass Works on Lot number Forty Two, on the North side of Talbot Road, in the Township of Cayuga, and County of Haldimand.

Whether or not this Cayuga glass house went into actual production and made use of the listed site, or whether the Government took advantage of section XVIII which reads: " . . . notwithstanding the privileges hereby conferred . . . [the Province] may at any time . . . make such addition . . . or . . . alteration . . . they . . . think proper, for affording . . . protection to the Public," and the subscription lists closed, are questions we cannot answer. If at some future date the books mentioned in section XIV are found, or Lot 42 is excavated, and such evidence shows that this house made even a single batch of glass, then this earliest of Cayuga glass works will deserve a place of honour as the second glass house in the Canadas.

In an effort to gather authentic data relative to glass making in the Cayuga area the author has been in touch with several persons. Two of these, M. R. Billings, D.D.S. and A. P. Stitt, reeve of the municipality of the village of Cayuga, have been especially helpful. Dr. Billings writes:

There was, however, another Glass Company given a charter in 1906 to make glass in Cayuga. Application was made to the Canadian Government by the American Plate Glass Company of Pittsburgh for a patent right to manufacture glass in Canada, and permission was granted on condition they build a factory, make glass and employ men from the locality. The factory was built here in Cayuga in 1906. It was called, I believe, the Cayuga Plate Glass Company. The material was obtained from what the local people called the sand plant, about three miles west of here. They did manufacture some glass, but I am led to believe that none was ever shipped out but was broken up and put back into the furnaces. . . . When I came to Cayuga in 1908 there was no activity around the factory excepting a night and day watchman. In 1912 the building was wrecked and sold locally, and the machinery was sold to the Pinkerton Glass Company of Thorold, Ontario.

Mr. Stitt writes:

Glass was manufactured in Cayuga approximately fifty years ago. The raw material was obtained . . . three and a half miles from Cayuga. The foundations of the plant, etc., are still there.

Thanks to these two gentlemen we have some knowledge of the second attempt at glass making at Cayuga, two names have been added to the list of Canadian glass houses. Indeed, Canadian glass houses seem to have sprung up everywhere in twentieth century Ontario.

20. The Consumers Glass Company Limited, Montreal (1913-)

A SHORT history of the Consumers Glass Company Limited of
Montreal is included in this work because of the several names under
which the various managements attempted the making of glass on a scale
to compete with imported as well as with native products.  We are indebted
for the following data to Mr. R. C. P. (Peter) Webster, Maitland, Ontario,
a major stockholder in the firm and the inventor of a system now used
to speed up production.

As far as can be ascertained, the parent firm of the present Consumers
Glass Company was the Atlas Glass Company.  This was formed by
experienced glass men who had been associated with the Diamond Flint
Glass Company of Montreal, the parent of the present Dominion Glass
Company Limited.  Our informant mentions a man named Pugh as
one of these.  (For earlier mention of Mr. Dave Pugh see chapter 12.)

The Atlas glass house consisted of a two furnace factory, the erection
of which was begun *circa* 1913.  Although this house purchased a site
and began a building, it did not produce glass.  The records show that
funds did not permit its completion.

The management, which consisted of men who knew they could make
glass if given the opportunity, raised sufficient funds for a second attempt
to complete the plant.  The new company was known as the Premier
Glass Company.  For a short time construction proceeded, and it was
hoped that the plant would begin operation.  As was the case with
many Canadian glass houses, the management of the almost defunct
glass house gained further financial support, and the Consumers Glass
Company Limited was incorporated on October 4, 1917, completed its
plant, and got under way.

In the beginning this house operated with hand-shops and semi-
automatic machines.  Later, like all other glass companies in Canada,
it adopted the fully automatic techniques in use today, and the glass blower
became unnecessary.  The early companies mentioned above manufactured glass bottles and containers, as does their modern successor.

21. PILKINGTON GLASS LIMITED, TORONTO
(England, 1826-, Canada, 1913-)

THE YEAR 1826 was of some importance in the world of glass. In that year the first of the Canadian glass houses, that at Mallorytown, was nearing completion or had gone into production (see chapter 1), and the firm of Pilkington Brothers Limited was founded in St. Helens, Lancashire, England. The Mallorytown house has had little or no effect on glass in Canada, other than to bequeath a small number of rare collector's items; but the English firm now plays a prominent part in supplying glass for Canadian buildings.

There have been many Canadian attempts to produce window glass of a type to meet foreign competition, the earliest being that of the old Ottawa Glass Works (see chapter 8). Later, the glass houses in Napanee (see chapter 4) and Cayuga (see chapter 19) tried and failed. Indeed, it was not until World War II that commercial glass of types known through the years as Crown, Cylinder, Cylinder Drawn, Cast and Rolled Plate, Table Cast, Flow, Twin Grinder, and now Float, were made successfully in Canada.

In former years a Canadian wishing to purchase flat, transparent sheets of glass for windows or mirrors, for framing pictures, or for any other purpose had to buy a foreign product. In the early 1940's, with imports curtailed by the activity of the German submarines, Pilkington Glass began to manufacture commercial window glass in Canada.

Thanks to Mr. J. C. Scarff, of Pilkington Glass Limited, Toronto, we have been supplied with a catalogue illustrating and listing the main steps in the development of sheet glass. Although several techniques for the making of sheet glass are quoted in our introduction, the following facts are of interest:

50 B.C. : Small panes and tiles of glass were made by the Egyptians and Phoenicians by direct casting.
250 A.D. : Crown Glass was discovered and made by the Syrians.
1100 A.D. : Cylinder blown glass was mentioned by the monk Theophilus.

1687        : The casting and rolling process for the manufacture of plate
              glass was invented in France by Bernard Perrot.
1910        : The Cylinder method was mechanised.
1913        : Fourcault, a Belgian, developed a method of drawing flat
              sheets of glass direct from the tank.
1920        : The continuous flow process was invented.
1925        : The continuous grinding and polishing machine was invented.
1937        : The twin grinding and polishing machine was invented.
1952        : Pilkington Brothers invented the float glass process.
1959        : Pilkington Brothers offered glass produced by the float process.

This list indicates remarkable progress in glass-making. The author can remember a time when art dealers purchased cases of specially picked glass sheets made in Belgium and England and discovered on opening them that only about fifty per cent could be used. The reason was that imperfect glass cast shadows and marks on paintings, watercolours and prints. Many modern glass products are inferior to antique prototypes, but sheet glass is not one of them.

## AUTHENTICATED SPECIMENS IN THE EDITH CHOWN PIERCE AND
## GERALD STEVENS COLLECTION OF EARLY CANADIAN GLASS,
### ROYAL ONTARIO MUSEUM

This Catalogue lists authenticated specimens in the most important public collection of early Canadian glass. Since this is a "living" collection, new acquisitions are added to it from time to time. In many cases the items listed have been mentioned in the text, but if not they may be examined in their permanent home, the Royal Ontario Museum, Queen's Park, Toronto, Ontario.

### I
### THE MALLORYTOWN GLASS WORKS, MALLORYTOWN, U.C. (ONTARIO)
*[circa* 1825, 1839-1840]

> BURNHAM BOWL (sugar bowl and cover)
> SHIPMAN VASE
> GUILD TUMBLER
> BATES PITCHER
> FLASK
> LARGE CHUNKS OF GLASS
> SHARDS (excavated on the site)

### II
### THE HAMILTON GLASS WORKS, HAMILTON, ONTARIO
[1865-1895]

4 GLASS SEALERS (preserve jars embossed "Hamilton Glass Works," complete with flat glass covers and iron clamps with thumb-screws.)
FREE BLOWN AMBER CUSPIDOR
AMBER CANE
AMBER WITCH BALL. (This was once owned by Mother Barnes, the celebrated "Witch of Plumb Hollow," in Leeds County, Ontario.)
BOTTLE (embossed "F. Riddell—Hamilton Glass Works")

### III
### THE BURLINGTON GLASS WORKS, HAMILTON, ONTARIO
[1875-1909]

FREE BLOWN PAPER WEIGHT (lily with "J. A. Johnson from Ettie Harris") by William (Billy) McGinnis
FREE BLOWN PAPER WEIGHT (lily with "Wm. H. Hunt, Hamilton, Ont.") by William McGinnis
FREE BLOWN PAPER WEIGHT (lily with "Mrs. Andrew Craig, Dresden, Ont.") by William McGinnis
BLOWN "BAND MASTER" GLASS CANE by George Mullin (presented by Mr. Louis N. Long)
FREE BLOWN PAPER WEIGHT by George Mullin
MULTI-COLOURED GLASS DRAPE by George Gardiner

2 L'ange Gardien Lamps and Shades (C. H. Binks & Co.)
3 Ornaments for Glass Drapes
Lamp Chimney (and 2 pieces to authenticate same)
Member's Badge (Glass Bottle Blowers Association)
Small Flint Glass Lamp (with applied handle)
Footed Flint Glass Lamp
2 Aquamarine Bottle Glass Alleys (or bottle stoppers)
Opal Pipe (milk glass)
Green Ringed Hat (tooth pick holder)
Flint Glass Standard Lamp (bull's eye)
Water Pitcher (engraved "M.G.", made for Mrs. Gardiner)
Pistol Bottle
Fish Scale Lamp and Crimped Shade
Milk Glass Lamp (bull's eye)
Flint Glass Hand Lamp (bull's eye)
Paper Weight Colours (glass sticks)
Jar (flint glass sealer, "Key" design, with metal cover)
Blue Glass Hat ("beaver" type)
Covered Sugar Bowl (opal)
Opal Salt Shaker (Princess Feather)
Glass Cane (ruby and white spirals)
Butter Dish and Cover (bull's eye)
Two Mould Pale Green Ink Bottle
Chunk of Pale Green Glass (excavated on the site)

IV

JOHN HERRING, GLASS-MAKER, NAPANEE, ONTARIO

[1881-1883]

5 Mercury Glass Candlesticks
3 Druggist's Jars
Cane
Free Blown Flint Glass Beaker
2 Large Chunks of Glass

V

THE TORONTO GLASS COMPANY, TORONTO

[1894-1900]

Free Blown Green Bottle Glass Paper Weight (Masonic) by Patrick
Wickham
Free Blown Green Bottle Glass Paper Weight ("L. Milne") by Patrick
Wickham
Free Blown Green Bottle Glass Paper Weight ("Della Hollyman") by
Patrick Wickham
Flint Glass Drape by James Canty

VI

BEAVER FLINT GLASS COMPANY, TORONTO

[1897-1948]

Jar (sealer type embossed with beaver)

## VII
### JEFFERSON GLASS COMPANY, TORONTO, ONTARIO
[*circa* 1912]

GOBLET (Crystal pattern)
2 FLINT GLASS EGG CUPS (in (Chippendale) Crystal pattern)

## VIII
### THE SYDENHAM (DOMINION) GLASS COMPANY LIMITED, WALLACEBURG, ONTARIO
[1894-----)

FREE BLOWN PAPER WEIGHT ("To Annie," for Annie St. Clair Campbell—Mrs. H. E. Dickenson) by Chester Jorrey, a pupil of George Mullin
FLINT GLASS PITCHER (nugget design)
FREE BLOWN PAPER WEIGHT, made for A. E. W. Kimmerly
LARGE CHUNK OF OPAL GLASS (obtained on the site)
LARGE CHUNK OF DEEP AMBER BOTTLE GLASS
BLOW PIPE (*circa* 1889)

## IX
### OTTAWA GLASS WORKS, POINTE À CAVAGNOL, C.E. (COMO, QUEBEC)
[1847-1855]

2 MEDICINE BOTTLES with labels (mould-blown bottle glass)
5 FREE BLOWN HAMPER BOTTLES (bottle glass—Mrs. Percy Band)
CHUNK OF GREEN GLASS (excavated on the site)

## X
### CANADA GLASS WORKS, HUDSON, QUEBEC
[1866-1871]

RIBBED AMBER HAND LAMP (with applied flint glass handle)
CHUNK OF GLASS (obtained on the site)

## XI
### JOHN C. SPENCE, MONTREAL, C.E. (QUEBEC)
[1854-?]

4 VIGIL LIGHTS (deep blue, ruby, light amber, olive green)

## XII
### THE FOSTER BROTHERS GLASS WORKS, ST. JOHNS, L.C. (QUEBEC)
[1855-1880]

2 PLAIN GOBLETS
WILLOW-COVERED BOTTLE
SODA BOTTLE (embossed "Foster Brothers St. Johns, C.E.")
DALY GOBLET (engraved "J. B. McD."—Jean Brodie McDougall)

## XIII
### EXCELSIOR GLASS CO., ST. JOHNS, P.Q.
[1879-1880]

FLINT GLASS BEAVER GOBLET (embossed "St. Jean Baptiste, Quebec, 24 Juin 1880")
GOBLET (engraved "Ottawa Exhibition.")

## XIV
### DOMINION GLASS COMPANY, MONTREAL
[The early Dominion Co., 1886-1898]

FREE BLOWN BLUE GLASS PAPER WEIGHT ("Alice") by Patrick Wickham

## XV
### DIAMOND FLINT GLASS CO., MONTREAL
[1901-1912]

FREE BLOWN PAPER WEIGHT ("K. Dentist")

## XVI
### THE NOVA SCOTIA GLASS COMPANY, TRENTON, N.S.
[1881-1892]

CHEESE DISH (engraved "Mrs. J. K. Stewart")
WATER PITCHER
CREAM PITCHER
GLASS HAT (moulded tumbler)
PRESERVE DISH
SUGAR BOWL
EGG CUP
WATER PITCHER
QUEEN VICTORIA CAKE PLATE (1837)
QUEEN VICTORIA PLATE (duplicate)
QUEEN VICTORIA PLATE (variant)

## XVII
### THE HUMPHREY GLASS WORKS, TRENTON, N.S., & MONCTON, N.B.
[1890-1914, N.S.; 1915-1920, N.B.]

GOBLET
FLINT GLASS CHAIN
BLOWN GLASS CANE
COMPORT (without cover)—Mrs. W. D. Ross*
OVAL CAKE PLATE (1000-eye)—Mrs. W. D. Ross*

---

*These two specimens of early Nova Scotia glass were presented to this Collection of the Royal Ontario Museum as this book goes to press. They are authenticated by Mrs. Ross, wife of the late Hon. W. D. Ross, Lieut.-Governor of Ontario, and daughter of the late Mr. George

FLINT GLASS COMPORT AND COVER (tassel and crest design)
PRESERVE DISH (tassel and crest design)
CREAM PITCHER (tassel and crest design)
SPOON HOLDER (tassel and crest design)
SUGAR BOWL AND COVER (tassel and crest design)
FLINT GLASS WATER PITCHER
METALLIC LABEL (small, advertisement and calendar)

## XVIII
### THE LAMONT (DIAMOND) GLASS COMPANY, TRENTON, N.S.
#### [1890-1902]

LARGE WATER PITCHER, FLINT GLASS
BOTTLE (embossed "W. H. Donovan")
FLINT GLASS PIPE
SPOON HOLDER (engraved "M.F."—Mary Fraser)
LAMP CHIMNEY (late type)
TUMBLER (etched or sand blasted design with the Lord's Prayer)
BLOWN GLASS CANE

## XIX
### GUNDY-CLAPPERTON & SONS LIMITED, TORONTO, ONTARIO
#### [1905-----]

"D" PATTERN CUT GLASS TUMBLER
4 GOBLETS (showing four steps of cut glass)

## XX
### CAYUGA PLATE GLASS COMPANY, CAYUGA, ONTARIO
#### [1835? 1906-1908]

CHUNK OF LIGHT GREEN GLASS (excavated on site)

---

Forrest Mackay, Nova Scotia industrialist, who founded the first steel forge of Canada at Trenton. An uncle of Mrs. Ross, Mr. Andrew Walker, secretary of the Nova Scotia Glass Company, presented a water jug to the mother of Mrs. Ross attributed to his company. Benjamin Humphrey ("of the flowing red moustache"), named his son Forrest for his friend, Mrs. Ross' father. As a young girl Mrs. Ross, and her sister, the late Mrs. F. N. G. Starr, frequently met the leading families in the Trenton glass companies, including Mr. William Godkin Beach, General Manager of the Nova Scotia Glass Company, and both the Humphrey and Lamont families. This authentication is confirmed by Miss Sarah Fraser, daughter of the late Hon. D. C. Fraser, onetime Lieut.-Governor of Nova Scotia, and sister of the Hon. Alastair Fraser, present Lieut.-Governor of Nova Scotia, and a niece of the late Mr. Harvey Graham of the Nova Scotia Glass Company.

# A SELECTED BIBLIOGRAPHY

*Encyclopaedia Britannica:* Fourteenth Edition.
    A striking picture of the advance in glass-making can be secured by comparing these editions: I (1768-1771); IV (1801-1810); VIII (1853-1860); XI (1910-1911); XIII (1923-1926).

*Colonial Advocate* (newspaper). York (Toronto), 1830.

Statutes of Upper Canada, 1835.

*Harper's Statistical Gazetteer of the World*, by J. Calvin Smith. New York, Harper & Brothers, 1855.

*Canada at the Universal Exhibition of 1855.* Toronto, John Lovell, 1856.

*The Canada Directory*, 1857-1858. Montreal, John Lovell, 1857.

Toronto Directories, 1837-1959.

Montreal Directories, 1869-1912.

Hamilton Directories, 1865-1910.

*Canada Classified Directory.* Montreal, John Lovell, 1865.

*Province of Ontario Gazetteer and Directory.* Toronto, Robertson & Cook, 1869.

*Products and Manufactures of the New Dominion*, by H. Beaumont Small. Ottawa, G. E. Desbarats, 1868.

*Statements relating to Trade, Navigation, Mining, etc., for 1867* by William J. Patterson. Montreal, Starke & Co., 1868.

*Canada Dominion Directory*, 1871.

*Gazetteer of British North America*, 1874, 1881, 1895.

*Year Book and Almanac of Canada*, 1876. Montreal and Ottawa, MacLean, Roger & Co.

*Home and Foreign Trade of Canada*, with *Annual Report of the Commerce of Montreal for 1880 to 1882*, by William J. Patterson. Montreal, D. Bentley & Co., 1883.

*Sketches of the Late Depression*, etc., by William Johnson. Montreal, J. Theo. Robinson, 1882.

*Ontario Gazetteer*, 1884-1885.

*A Cyclopaedia of Canadian Biography*, edited by George Maclean Rose. Toronto, Rose Publishing Company, 1886.

*A Chronology of Montreal*, etc., by Frederick William Terrill. Montreal, John Lovell & Son, 1893.

*Might 5 Cities Business Directory.* Toronto, The Might Directory Co., 1895.

*Toronto Directory*, 1897. Toronto, The Might Directory Co.

*History of the County of Lennox and Addington*, by Walter S. Herrington. Toronto, The Macmillan Co., 1913.

*Glass Making in England*, by T. H. Powell. London, 1932.

*A History of English and Irish Glass*, by W. A. Thorpe. London, The Medici Society, 1929.

*American Glass*, by George S. and Helen McKearin. New York, Crown Publishers, 1941.

*Special Price List of Historical Flasks and Bottles*, by George S. McKearin. Hoosick Falls, N.Y., McKearin's Antiques.

*Glass*, by E. Barrington Haynes. London, Penguin Books, 1948. A Pelican Book.

*Handbook of Early American Pressed Glass Patterns*, by Ruth Webb Lee.
*Sandwich Glass Handbook*, by Ruth Webb Lee.
*Victorian Glass Handbook*, by Ruth Webb Lee.
*Antique Fakes and Reproductions*, by Ruth Webb Lee.
     These titles were privately published by Ruth Webb Lee at Northboro, Mass., U.S.A.
*Milk Glass*, by E. McCamly Belknap.   New York, Crown Publishers, 1949.
*Wallaceburg, The Glasstown since 1891*.  Wallaceburg, Ontario, Dominion Glass Company Limited.
*Antiques Magazine*, August, 1955, article by H. A. Boire.   (This suggests the importance of Mallorytown glass.)
*Canadian Glass: A Footnote to History*, by Edith Chown Pierce.   Toronto, The Ryerson Press, Privately Printed, 1954.
*Historic Kingston*, No. 3.  (A paper on "Early Canadian Glass" by Gerald Stevens).  Kingston, Kingston Historical Society, 1954.
*The Edith Chown Pierce and Gerald Stevens Collection of Early Canadian Glass* (an historical and descriptive catalogue), by Gerald Stevens, with Introduction by A. D. Tushingham.  Toronto, Royal Ontario Museum, 1957.
*The Canadian Collector*, by Gerald Stevens.   Toronto, The Ryerson Press, 1957.
*Nova Scotia Museum Newsletter*, vol. 2, no. 3: "The Trenton Glass Works," by George MacLaren.   Halifax, N.S., April 1958.
*Early Glass Houses of Nova Scotia*, by Lorne Pierce.   Toronto, The Ryerson Press, 1958.  Limited to 250 copies.
*Float Glass* (brochure).   Toronto, Pilkington Glass Limited, 1959.
*On the Making of Stained Glass Windows* (brochure).   Toronto, Robert McCausland Limited.
*The Canadian Pottery and Glass Gazette*.   Toronto, Publishers Limited.
*Collectors' Luck, Canada and Europe*, by F. St. George Spendlove (especially chap. 10, "Glass Through the Ages").   Toronto, The Ryerson Press, 1960.

Newspapers, directories, almanacs, early catalogues, local and parish histories, vital statistics records, company records, letters, diaries and account books in college and public libraries and archives.